Differentiated Instruction Using Technology

A Guide for Middle and High School Teachers

Amy Benjamin

EYE ON EDUCATION
6 DEPOT WAY WEST, SUITE 106
LARCHMONT, NY 10538
(914) 833–0551
(914) 833–0761 fax
www.eyeoneducation.com

Library of Congress Cataloging-in-Publication Data

Benjamin, Amy, 1951-
Differentiated instruction using technology : a guide for middle and high school teachers / Amy Benjamin.
          p. cm.
Includes bibliographical references.
ISBN 1-930556-83-7
1. Individualized instruction—Computer-assisted instruction. 2. Middle school education—Computer-assisted instruction. 3. Education, Secondary—Computer-assisted instruction. I. Title.
LB1031.B464 2005
371.39′4—dc22

                                        2004028102

10 9 8 7 6

Editorial and production services provided by
Richard H. Adin Freelance Editorial Services
52 Oakwood Blvd., Poughkeepsie, NY 12603-4112
(914-471-3566)

Also Available from EYE ON EDUCATION

**Handbook on Differentiated Instruction
for Middle and High Schools**
Sheryn Spencer Northey

**Differentiated Instruction:
A Guide for Middle and High School Teachers**
Amy Benjamin

**Differentiated Instruction:
A Guide for Elementary School Teachers**
Amy Benjamin

Writing in the Content Areas, Second Edition
Amy Benjamin

**What Every Teacher Needs to Know
About Assessment, Second Edition**
Leslie Wilson

**Applying Standards-based Constructivism:
A Two-Step Guide for Motivating Middle and High School Students**
Flynn, Mesibov, Vermette, & Smith

**Helping Students Graduate:
A Strategic Approach to Dropout Prevention**
Jay Smink and Franklin Schargel

**Socratic Seminars and Literature Circles
for Middle and High School English**
Victor and Marc Moeller

**Using Data to Improve Student Learning
in Middle Schools**
Victoria Bernhardt

**At-Risk Students:
Reaching and Teaching Them Second Edition**
Richard Sagor and Jonas Cox

**Constructivist Strategies:
Meeting Standards and Engaging Adolescent Minds**
Foote, Vermette, and Battaglia

Acknowledgments

I wish to express many thanks to Tom March, creator of Web–Flow, and co-developer, along with Bernie Dodge at San Diego State University, of what has come to be known as the Web Quest. I would also like to thank the editors of Quia.com for giving me permission to include their pages. In addition, Becky Fisher, Michael Muir, and Kathryn Schladweiler, gave me very helpful comments and direction when this book was in development. Many thanks to my colleague Maura Koch at Hendrick Hudson High School for her tireless work on RxWrite. And, once again, I thank my publisher, Robert N. Sickles, for his expertise in managing this project.

Meet the Author

Amy Benjamin is the author of several other books for educators published by Eye On Education: *Writing in the Content Areas; An English Teacher's Guide to Performance Tasks and Rubrics: Middle School/High School; Differentiated Instruction: A Guide for Middle and High School Teachers; and Differentiated Instruction: A Guide for Elementary School Teachers.* Amy trains teachers in school districts across the country in English Language Arts and differentiated instruction. She is president of the Assembly for the Teaching of English Grammar, whose goal is to educate teachers about current research and to make grammar instruction come alive in the classroom. Amy teaches English at Hendrick Hudson High School in Montrose, New York. She has been awarded Excellence in Teaching awards from Tufts University and Union College, and has served as a model teacher for the New York State Education Department.

TABLE OF CONTENTS

User's Guide

The purpose of this book is to help you advance your teaching skills by marshaling technology, mostly computer technology, to meet the different needs and learning styles of your students. My hope is that by reading this book you will have a better idea about how to modernize your pedagogy and manage the complexities of differentiated instruction.

If you are a novice at differentiated instruction, the first and second chapters will bring you up to speed. Chapter 1 presents an overview the foundations of differentiated instruction (DI), and Chapter 2 gives you a detailed lexicon. In both chapters, as you would expect, I've included the necessary foundational information that brings technology into the DI paradigms.

This book may be used as a primer on DI, but it is not a primer on the use of technology in the classroom. However, many of the Web sites listed in the Appendix speak to teachers on a basic, very user-friendly level. I'm sure that if you jump in, you'll find that you can navigate that information quite well, and you'll be doing things with technology that you never dreamed possible.

Chapter 2 gives you working definitions for terms used in conversations about DIs and technology in education. You will find this chapter rich in information and implied ideas about the possibilities of using technology to differentiate instruction. Think of this chapter as supermarket aisles. You have a list of what you came into the store for, but you're happy to toss appealing items into your cart as you go along.

Chapters 3, 4, and 5 give you detailed information about the mainstays of DI: tiered tasks, unit menus, learning centers, and stations. Here, you'll find suggestions for giving students choices based on their learning styles, abilities, and interests. I hope you find that these suggestions and explanations are appropriate for the secondary level. One of the reasons why I've written this book is because I understand the mindset of secondary teachers, being one myself, and I believe that DI for secondary classrooms is not the same as it is for elementary classrooms.

One of the ways in which secondary teachers tend to differ from elementary teachers, and rightly so, is that on the secondary level we have a great deal of whole-class instruction, and we rely heavily on traditional tests for assessment. Chapters 6 and 7 show you how DI comports with whole-class instruction and how to use technology to differentiate traditional tests by creating test banks and adaptations.

Chapter 8 describes how E-communications—whole-class, student-to-student, and teacher-to-student-to-teacher—work in state-of-the-art classrooms, even if those classrooms and communities don't have state-of-the-art equipment. In this chapter, I explain how teacher-made Web sites can be used as more than just bulletin boards, and how students can use their Internet language to advance their academic thinking.

Chapter 9 explains how prescriptive lessons work: You archive your own lessons and put them on a class Web site or hotlist, along with the links that you choose, to reinforce and advance skills. Chapter 10 explains how to use Quia (www.quia.com) to create and find all kinds of puzzles and games that reinforce learning.

Chapter 11 explains how to use data to make decisions about how to differentiate instruction, and Chapter 12 presents detailed models of DI in practice. Included are WebQuests and hotlists. The Appendices give you some interesting resources and helpful articles.

With both DI and teaching with technology, your role as teacher is ever-changing as you adapt. What remains anchored are the essential questions and the processes of learning how to learn. With these in place, and with flexibility, inquisitiveness, and a pioneer spirit, you can keep things interesting for everyone. That is what this book is about.

Web sites are constantly being updated and changed. Some of the Web sites referenced in this book may have moved, or may display content that differs from that presented here.

1

Foundations

An Overview of Differentiated Instruction

Differentiated instruction (DI) is a broad term. It refers to a variety of classroom practices that allow for differences in students' learning styles, interests, prior knowledge, socialization needs, and comfort zones. The standards tell us what students need to know and be able to do. Differentiated instruction practices help to get students there, while at the same time teaching them *how* to learn in a meaningful way.

In its modern application, a differentiated classroom is widely heterogeneous, dynamic, purposeful, and intense. On the secondary level, few classes are differentiated all of the time. Whole-class instruction prevails much of the time, as new information is introduced. Differentiation can come in at any point in the learning cycle.

The pedagogical theory that guides differentiation is constructivism: *the belief that learning happens when the learner makes meaning out of information.* That may sound too self-evident to deserve mention. Of course, learning involves making meaning out of information. What else would learning involve? Well, if you've ever seen a kid memorize definitions for a list of vocabulary words without having the slightest idea of how to use, or any intention of using, those words in context, then you know what learning is *not*: We do *not* know the meaning of a word, the significance of a historical event, or the applications of a formula just because we have memorized a set of words. That is why the first step toward DI is knowing what understanding means.

Differentiated instruction, when done well, has a side benefit: Because students may have learned about different exemplars of a concept, they learn from each other when the class comes together for presentation. The concept may be something like this: "Geographical features determine economy and lifestyle." A middle school American studies class is divided into five groups, each group applying the concept to a region of the United States. After their projects are completed, each group will present to the class; thus, time is used efficiently for durable learning of an essential concept.

The mainstays of DI are flexible grouping, unit menus, and tiered tasks. Flexible grouping distinguishes true DI classes from those that are de facto "in-class tracking." The latter results in a rigidly stratified class in which some students feel like second-class citizens. Flexible grouping allows for a healthy socialization among members of the class. Groups can form in various configurations. Sometimes it's appropriate to group students by ability, as demonstrated through some sort of assessment. Ability groups can be homogeneous or heterogeneous. Other times, groups can form on the basis of interest, with students choosing particular topics. Students can form their own groups, or groups can be assigned randomly. What's important is that a differentiated classroom is a dynamic place, in which students often work collaboratively and have some choice and control of their own learning, if not the content itself, then certainly the process. Although all students need to show competency on the standards, they can sometimes find different ways to show what they know. I believe strongly, and the learning experiences in this book will show, that reading and writing needs to be emphasized in all subject areas. Differentiation absolutely does not mean that we teach *around* literacy skills, especially for special education students.

Unit menus are lists of choices. Some teachers set these up as *choice boards* or *task cards*. A well-designed unit menu presents an array of processes and assessments, all of which would take comparable amounts of time and effort to complete, while satisfying the same essential questions and meeting the same learning goals. This book presents numerous examples of unit menus that employ technology in the mix. You may be used to using unit menus as assessment choices. Unit menus can also be offered prior to whole-class instruction to establish a knowledge base on which students can build the details that you will be teaching. If you do this, you will have built-in *experts* as you teach the unit. You can also offer unit menus as the process for learning. After you've instructed the whole class, you can offer a menu of choices in ways to gather and synthesize information. Then, you could give a traditional test to the whole class. Unit menus capitalize on learning style. They say to the student: "Here are some ways that you can make this information yours in the way that you learn best. We are all learning the same information, but we can learn it, or show that we know it, in different ways." Again, the language and literacy skills of the subject should be there, and all items on the unit menu should reach toward the standards.

Tiered tasks are leveled according to sophistication. Usually, there are three tiers. Students choose, or are assigned to, a particular tier. As you will see in the examples, the three tiers are not just increasingly complex versions of the same task; that would be demeaning to the students with the least demanding task. Rather, they are different *kinds* of tasks, but each should involve the same amount of time and effort, while satisfying the same essential questions and learning goals. Designing tiered tasks requires imagination, a variety of resources, and a thorough knowledge of the standards. The key to successful tiering is to balance fairness (of grading) with appropriateness (of task). You may have read of differentiating being "invisible" to the students. This means that students don't feel that they or others are "getting off easy" or made to do "harder work" for the same grade. In elementary grades, this invisibility may be easier to achieve than it would be at the secondary level. For that reason, I always recommend that students have a choice in the tiered tasks, and that the grade is adjusted, reflecting the complexity of the task.

Technology in Education

The thought of bringing more technology into our classrooms, especially in terms of differentiation—an already mind-boggling thought—is overwhelming. No one could have prepared me for the tidal wave of information on the Internet available for teachers. As you learn about what's out there, you will surely feel amazed and invigorated. But you can also expect to feel intimidated and maybe a little lost. It's like trying to take a drink of water from a fire hydrant.

What are teachers around the country actually doing with technology? It may seem that more is happening than actually is. I run workshops in very resource-rich districts in major cities and affluent suburbs around the country. I learn a lot about what's available and how state-of-the-art educators are using it. But I also notice many teachers' and district Web sites that are just announcement boards or on-screen workbook pages. This book is about bringing technology to your classroom in a way that truly enriches communication and broadens a student's world.

You may be quite sophisticated in your use of technology, but you haven't really thought about it in terms of differentiation. You won't need the glossaries and introductory explanations in this book that give the basics of applications and the Internet. You may want to see how you can use your Web site to provide prescriptive lessons based on work that your students e-mail you. You may be interested in setting up tiered WebQuests, or tailoring your favorite WebQuests for different levels. You may not have thought about using blogging as an assessment, or having your students use their e-speak to transition into academic language.

You may have practiced differentiation with some tiered tasks or unit menus, but have stayed away from technology except for some basic applications that you learned a few years ago. I suggest that you start to include some technology-assisted presentations on PowerPoint in your unit menus, think about how you can make instructive use of word processing, try a WebQuest or two, start taking student work through e-mail and dabble in on-screen feed-back, maybe advance from paper portfolios to Webfolios.

If you are a novice at both differentiation and technology, you are in a good position to put both to use at the same time. I've included some vignettes showing how teachers like you put their feet in the water, implementing some simple but very effective differentiated structures that use easy applications of technology. You will be surprised, when you look at some Internet sites, such as MarcoPolo.com, EdHelper.com, MoneyInstructor.com, Myschoolonline.com, or Thirteen.org, at how much has already been done for you! If nothing else, you'll find more lesson plans, teaching tips, professional workshops, and accessible resources for educators than you ever dreamed possible.

Technology, whether that means a sharp pencil or the most sophisticated computer, should fulfill a need that a nontech or low-tech tool will not fill. Computers are not a fad in education, but we can make the mistake of under using them by treating them as fancy workbooks. We may be used to thinking of computers as *tools*, but they are more than that: Computers are environments for communication and learning, for work and play.

When it comes to DI, we don't want to put kids on computers just to keep them occupied while we work with other groups. We want computers to enhance instruction, not just parallel it. That is why, though there are countless programs and Web sites out there that offer *workbook on-screen* experiences, I will not be directing you to them. Even when it comes to graphic organizers, which you can download in profusion, it is my opinion that we can draw our own Venn diagrams and T charts. The same is true with educational games: Although they are useful in providing reinforcement and review of concepts taught in class, I would like to direct you to uses of technology that are truly constructivist, where students engage in higher level thinking, meaningful communication, creation of original work, and problem solving in nonlinear ways. Think of technology as a means of providing *support*, *opportunity*, and *clarity*.

Working Collegially

Recently, I was in my school's computer lab with a ninth-grade class. I wanted to set up an intraclass chat room for them, and my plan wasn't working because some unnamed force had disabled the e-mail function (so that students wouldn't waste computer lab time with frivolous e-mail). Frustrated, I do what I always do in school whenever technology doesn't yield to my command: I asked the kids for help. Stephen, one of my ninth-grade students, showed me how to set up a group in Yahoo, and away we went on our e-chat.

A rookie teacher using the computer behind me looked a little baffled at my surprise at being able to set up this Yahoo group. "I didn't know to do this. Isn't this great?" I remarked. This young teacher may have been trying to disguise his surprise at my incompetence, but he was looking at me as if I'd told him that I didn't know how to make a peanut butter and jelly sandwich. This got me to thinking: Our young colleagues, like our students, are as used to e-communications and e-learning as we veteran teachers are to keeping a grade book by hand. We, however, have much to offer them in terms of managing multileveled, heterogeneous classes. What we know about classroom management, they know about technology. This is where we need to collaborate. As never before, novices and veteran teachers have much to offer each other.

Differentiated instruction is a lot of work, as is finding resources on the Internet and setting up a classroom Web site with prescriptive lessons. You don't have to go it alone in either endeavor. Ideally, departments and clusters of like-minded teachers can put together all kinds of concept-based learning experiences and even keep track of what students have already done from one class and year to the next. Naturally, building a collaborative faculty is the job of leaders. Curriculum coordinators and department heads need to match teachers to one another to create in-house libraries. If teachers work collaboratively, schools can establish coherent structures for using technology to differentiate instruction.

Features of Technology that Support Differentiated Instruction

The purpose of this book is not just to encourage the use of computers, telecommunications, and multimedia; my purpose, more specifically, is to show how DI can be accomplished through technology. Once we understand what DI is all about, why shouldn't we use technology to get us there?

- ◆ *Privacy*. A thorny problem in DI is how to protect the self esteem of the student who is working on the least sophisticated task. Not only does computer work afford privacy, but it is possible to give the least sophisticated group the most sophisticated technology with which to accomplish their task. Technology is always to be thought of as just one of many options for learning.

- ◆ *Collaboration and communication skills*. Although some people are concerned that computers are isolating, computers can help us bond as a class, forming a learning community. When students work in clusters, when they e-conference and e-mail, when they strategize a complex problem and share their findings, the best kinds of educational communication take place. As teachers, we need to design learning experiences that foster communication to strengthen learning.

♦ *Organization.* If you are going to differentiate instruction, you are going to have to count on your students to do a lot of the organizational work that you might do yourself (for them) in whole-class instruction. Programs such as Inspiration Software produce outlines and graphic organizers that help students be independent. Tables, databases, and spreadsheets help them document their observations. And, of course, e-files and folders are easier to keep track of than papers (assuming proper backup procedures have been followed!).

♦ *Learning styles and sensory learning.* Computers allow for visual, auditory, and social learning. The interplay and possibilities of learning through words, images, and sounds, as well as the availability of review, make computers extremely effective as learning tools.

♦ *Choices.* The sheer extravagance of information available on the Internet and in software at all different levels of depth and complexity makes us understand the usefulness of computers in DI.

♦ *Authentic learning.* Differentiated instruction tends to be projects-based, favoring authentic, constructivist activities over traditional testing (although traditional testing is still, more than ever, an important component).

In addition to the above, we acknowledge the motivational value of computers for most students. Computers are how they hear and find their music, talk with their friends, get information, shop, and entertain themselves. Many, if not most, teenagers do the majority of their reading on computers. They participate in an informal language community called e-speak. This language is not, as some people think, a degeneration of English language conventions: Rather, e-speak is one evolution of language, a cross between writing and speech. It is writing because, obviously, it uses symbols rather than voice. But, unlike writing, e-speak is quick and evanescent. The receiver is not expecting the same deliberation and adherence to rules that is normally expected in written communication. In that sense, e-speak is more like spontaneous speech. Actually, it's a transcribed telephone call, a new form of the English language. Don't expect it to go away.

No Teacher Left Behind

Technology has always revolutionized societies. Revolutions always have unexpected consequences. When revolutions happen, the younger generation always outpaces the older generation. As teachers, we can't be the last to catch on; we have to be willing to learn from our students, to accept their world. If we don't, if we teachers leave ourselves behind, then what we have to offer students will be irrelevant to the world that they are to inherit. They will know that this gap exists well before we do.

We have as much as educators ever have had to offer our students in terms critical thinking, love of the beautiful and the complex, unlocking meaning, perceiving subtlety, communicating clearly, transcending the obvious. But if we teach in the 21st century with the equipment of the 20th century, then we will mismatch ourselves to our students. Teaching with technology is transformative. It is we who must transform. Society already has.

As for differentiation, we need to understand how constructivist pedagogy undergirds teaching that results in durable, meaningful learning. Constructivists follow these practices:

♦ Teaching subject area content and simultaneously teaching students how to learn. The content and the metacognition form parallel teaching: Students learn what they are learning, as well as how they are learning it. The former is likely to be forgotten as way leads on to way in life; the latter endures as a life skill.

♦ Encouraging students to be autonomous learners, bringing new information into their experience so that it makes sense.

♦ Using a variety of media, but not losing sight of reading, writing, and communicating in the language of the subject area.

♦ Respecting and using the students' home language to help them integrate academic language.

♦ Teaching organically, allowing for teachable moments and inquiry that comes out of authentic student interest and open-ended questions.

♦ Teaching cumulatively, thinking of the student's education as ongoing, rather than limited to *units* that *end* with a test.

♦ Encouraging elaboration and transcendence of the obvious.

♦ Welcoming productive digressions.

♦ Seeking understanding through metaphor.

Matching Tech to Teacher

Your home technology may be mismatched to the technology available to you at school. Your school's technology, and the people who run it, may be a source of great frustration to you. There may be a mismatch between the home technology of your students and that which is available to them at school, as well as a wide variety of quality of home technology. You may be surprised to find that parents are not as trustful of the benefits of the Internet as you are.

In any case, from now until the end of your teaching career (or working career, for that matter), get prepared to advance your skills. How can you do this? A lot of technology skills can be self taught, some of it the hard way. (Ask anyone who encounters a tech crisis at home.) Your district probably offers courses and workshops, or would be willing to do so in response to collective interest. Use your colleagues. If you have children who are old enough to talk, ask them. And ask your students.

You may have one computer in your room. If you don't have a projector, your one computer is probably going to be used by only you most of the time. You obviously can't have more than two students huddled around a single computer. If you have a projection device, you can use your one computer effectively for whole class instruction. Smart Boards and other such devices allow notes to be saved and distributed; there are advantages and disadvantages to this. You may have a cluster of computers in your room or a nearby location. Students can rotate to clusters to work together or independently. You may have access to a computer lab, a location which will accommodate a whole class. Your students will have home access (or not) in varying degrees of sophistication. The less their home access to computers, the more urgent your imperative to get them to use computers and the Internet. Encourage use of the public library.

Computers give us access to more information, making it more necessary than ever to use critical thinking skills to evaluate and synthesize sources. But no one ever said that computers give us less work. (Well, maybe someone said that, but that person is wrong. Computers make life more interesting, but they do give us more to do and be distracted by.)

Use what you have. Don't wait for the *perfect* technological equipment and services to come along before having your own Web site, assigning and creating WebQuests, or welcoming e-communications as part of your classroom offerings.

Models of Differentiated Instruction

Differentiation can be overt or subtle. You are probably already doing it. Any time everyone in the class is not expected to do the same thing in the same way, and show what they know in the same way, that's a form of differentiation.

One popular way of viewing DI has been developed by Carol Ann Tomlinson (1999). This is to think of differentiation on three variables of the learning cycle: content, process, and product. Differentiating for content means that everyone is learning the same concept (geography affects culture) but using different exemplars to get there. Differentiating for process means that everyone is learning the same concept, but using different modalities to make the information stick. And differentiating for product means that that students have different ways of showing what they know. To call your instruction differentiated, you don't have to differentiate on all three of these variables. You make decisions based on your own teaching abilities, resources, and the needs of your students.

A word about the limits of DI: In my opinion, structures that may work well on the elementary level do not work as well in later years. Students become increasingly aware of equity issues in how they are graded for what they have done. Students and parents are likely to resent different grading scales for students in the same class. If the so-called differentiated class functions as no more than in-class tracking, that is not going to work well on the secondary level.

The history of DI (short history that it is) is mostly in elementary classrooms, extended into middle school. In this book, and in my other book, *Differentiated Instruction: A Guide for Middle and High School Teachers*, we're looking at what's going to work in high school and middle school classrooms (Benjamin, 2002). Secondary teachers tend to be subject-oriented in training and interest. Our time constraints are more rigid than those of elementary school teachers: when the bell rings, that's it. Plus, our time is cut short by attendance-taking and start-up tasks. We may collaborate with a special education teacher, but, that teacher usually doesn't have subject area expertise. For these reasons, secondary teachers need their own kind of training in differentiation, and what they practice is going to be much more limited than what you might find in the lower grades.

Differentiated instruction is complex. For it to work, resources need to be available. These resources include a variety of reading materials, supportive learning aids, the architectural structures (such as study carrels) necessary for students to work quietly, and reliable computers. Additionally, human resources must be available. Most elementary classes have at least some teacher aide time, but few high school classes do. If we expect students to have adequate access to teachers, we need smaller class sizes for differentiation than we would with a class in which everyone is expected to listen to the same lecture. Librarians need to keep informed and be available. We can't expect to do things differently if our resources remain the same, nor can we expect an elementary school model to become a high school model without substantial alterations.

I think the best place to look for differentiation on the secondary level is an art class. The studio art teacher delivers whole class instruction, showing a model of a particular technique; let's say shading with charcoal. The students execute that technique but they may choose their own subject. Their work is evaluated against criteria, but usually some reward is given for noted improvement. Students are expected not only to produce art—not anything they feel like, in any way they want—but to demonstrate proper protocols for handling materials and proper language. Their work is usually evaluated on the basis of a portfolio; they are not evaluated on attempts that ended up in the trash basket.

Lower levels attract students with a casual interest in art as well as serious art students. Upper levels attract mostly the latter, and the criteria are more stringent and more based on product, less on effort.

Finally, administrators need to be involved in the training process so that they can be sources of support and agents of change. They need to know not only what differentiation might look like on the secondary level, but also how to bring staff members together to facilitate it. Administrators tend to want differentiation to happen, but they really need to know something about what they can do to midwife the transition. This can mean helping teachers know what is going on outside of individual classrooms so that efforts can be combined. It can mean hooking teachers up with the right consultants, who understand *secondary* education. It can mean attending workshops along with teachers, organizing and participating in study groups, being knowledgeable about models in other schools. Without administrative support, we can expect many teachers to abandon their attempts at differentiation, finding it too unwieldy.

If you're working from a textbook that has an instructor's guide and ready-made tests, you can forego philosophy and reflection. But if you are blazing new trails based on the students and your own evolving interests as a secondary school teacher or administrator, you may find that it's easy to fall away from bedrock principles that should be guiding your day-to-day practice. For this reason, I'll launch you on your way through the rest of this book with some essential questions.

Essential Questions for Teachers About Differentiated Instruction

Do students have any choice in what they are learning, or in how they go about learning it, or in how they show what they know? Where would choices be appropriate? What is nonnegotiable in the learning process?

How am I addressing the different needs, interests, learning styles, and abilities of my students?

If learning isn't happening for some students, how can I go about teaching them in an alternate way?

How am I addressing the needs of students who are ready to advance?

Are there technological solutions or enhancements to what is being taught?

Summary

We should differentiate instruction when doing so would be the best means to solve a problem. We should use technology in education when doing so would be the best means to solve a problem. Technology is the best way that I know of to differentiate instruction because technology facilitates classroom management, provides an infinite variety of resources, and affords privacy.

Because of limited equipment and limited experience, to use technology to differentiate instruction we must work collegially as never before. We need to collaborate on class, departmental, interdisciplinary, and schoolwide Web sites that function as in-class libraries and communications centers. We need to attend workshops together and present a unified need for software, hardware, and training. We need to make intelligent, informed, open-minded decisions about what should be blocked and what should be accessible to our students on school computers. Finally, we need to choose activities that don't just pass the time by providing on-screen seatwork, but that advance higher level thinking.

2

The Language of Differentiated Instruction

Because differentiated instruction is broad based, much of its language is heard elsewhere in educational conversation. Presented here are some working definitions to help you navigate though this book.

Academic Computer Literacy: When we think of computer literacy, we may be thinking of the ability to use common software applications such as word processing, presentations, computations, data management, and the Internet. Efficient reading of a Web site calls for processing multiple messages and images which may appear side by side.

A student learning academic computer literacy is developing the skills to

- Locate information on the Internet by using search engines and links

- Skim for main ideas

- Scan for specific facts

- Use multiple sources to answer a question or pursue a topic

- Use various print and online reference tools

- Locate and interpret maps

- Interpret graphs and other nonprint layouts

- Organize data: Here is where to

  - Access and

  - Evaluate the validity and applicability of sources:

Here is where domain considerations come in. An ".edu" domain will assure that the site is connected to an educational institution, usually a college. Other institutional domains include government (.gov) and military (.mil). The ".org" domains used to be more reliable than they are now, but now with the open access policy on the .org domain, you have to be more selective. Although ".com" domains run the gamut, from highly respectable to the incoherent musings of a teenaged maniac, you might want to include some guidelines on how to evaluate a source for credibility on its subject.

♦ Present and explain information in a visually pleasing and targeted way

Alternative Assessments: Also known as authentic assessments or performance tasks, *alternative assessments* are ways, other than the traditional pencil-and-paper tests, for students to show what they know. Written reports can be considered alternative assessments when they are something other than traditional essays or straightforward reports (which are usually not good assessments anyway, because they are so easily plagiarized). Many teachers bring in the various forms of intelligence when drawing up alternative assessments. In teaching writing for social communication, a teacher might have students write thank-you notes or invitations, using desktop publishing to enhance the message with the design elements. For science, it might be caring for a plant or pet and keeping a log of its needs and progress, using Excel to track the data. Art and music, almost entirely based on authentic assessment, use technology to produce the final product.

Here are some questions that will help you recognize authentic assessment and show how technology fits in:

♦ Does the task arise from the need to solve a real problem? Will technology make the solving of the problem more efficient?

♦ Does the task require planning, communication, research, or cross-disciplinary thinking? Will a graphic organizer be the best way to chart a plan? Will e-mail be one way to communicate? Will the Internet be the best way to find this information?

♦ Is the task memorable? Can technology reinforce the learning?

♦ Did the student have any input in the nature of the task?

♦ Can the task be evaluated against a rubric?

♦ Does the task have real-world connections? If so, can technology make the connections stronger?

♦ Will every student produce the same exact product? Is there a way for technology to individualize the product?

♦ Is the task completed over time? Can technology be used to track progress or communicate with the teacher regarding progress?

♦ Will the task enable the student to better understand her own learning needs? Can technology be used to help the student reflect?

♦ Will the task capitalize on the student's strengths and strengthen her weaknesses?

It is not necessary for a task to meet all, or even most, of these questions to be considered authentic. The key is that authentic assessments give the student a sense of ownership of the learning and the product; whereas, inauthentic tasks have the feel of *doing something for the teacher*. It's important to note that the use of technology alone does not constitute authenticity or effectiveness. A spelling test, for example, based on a given list of words that seems random to the students, would be considered an inauthentic task. To assess spelling authentically, you would have to look at how students spell the words that they are actually writing, how they form patterns among words, and whether or not they at least have a logical, phonetic approach to spelling.

Anchor Activities: Anchor activities are activities that students can do by themselves: reading a book of choice, browsing through a Web site, journal writing, learning logs, graphic organizers, e-mailing and participating in threaded discussions online, and reviewing and reinforcing material that needs to be memorized. Typically, students have anchor activities to do at their own desks, in the library media center, or at the computer lab.

Asynchronous Communication: This occurs when people communicate outside of real time, as in some forms of e-conferencing, where people post to an e-board and then read the other postings at different times. We could say that letter-writing of the old-fashioned kind is asynchronous communication (as would posting to a real bulletin board, for that matter), whereas a telephone conversation happens in real time.

Bloom's Taxonomy: When educators say "Bloom," they are referring to six levels of learning, from most basic (knowledge) to most sophisticated (evaluation). Bloom's taxonomy (often referred to as simply *Bloom*) establishes this hierarchy:

In explaining how the hierarchy works, we've used "state government" as the topic:

1. *Knowledge.* The learner has the information. She knows who plays the key roles in her state capital. We acquire this level of learning by using the appropriate resources to answer straightforward questions: dictionaries, encyclopedias, atlases, and almanacs provide basic information. Students tend to copy or recite this information, but this knowledge should not be mistaken for the higher levels of learning. Often, we hear teachers lament that students plagiarize, cutting and pasting whole swatches of information from the Internet. Perhaps this occurs because the task itself required no more than basic knowledge of a subject. If we ask students to put the knowledge in another form: construct an outline or graphic or-

ganizer, for example, then blatant plagiarism becomes less of a problem.

2. *Comprehension.* The learner understands the information. She understands what her legislators and state committees can do. Assuming that the student has located certain information, she can show comprehension by putting it in her own words, by constructing questions, by having conversations.

3. *Application.* The learner can use the information. She can write to her state representatives, expressing her opinion or asking for assistance on appropriate matters. Most government sites include e-mail addresses.

4. *Analysis.* The learner can take apart and put together the information. She can identify the parts of a particular problem that could be solved by action by the state legislature. She can understand and proceed on their response. This level of understanding can be expressed in the form of a flow chart done in PowerPoint.

5. *Synthesis.* The learner can bring together disparate information. Having received a response from her legislator, she can propose another solution based on information from another source. She can compare and contrast different kinds of problems, finding similarities in seemingly unlike things and differences in seemingly like things. She can express these relationships in Venn diagrams.

6. *Evaluation.* The learner can make judgments based on criteria. She can compare and contrast various solutions, and can decide which is best in terms of cost, feasibility, popularity, environmental impact, and other factors.

Some teachers differentiate instruction according to the taxonomy. They may begin every task with a *Bloom verb*. If students were learning about the solar system, they could make PowerPoint presentations and documents that look like this:

Level One. Name the nine planets and give one fact about each. Decide what kinds of facts you want to give. You may decide to give facts about size, distance from the sun, distance from Earth, number of satellites (moon), or where the planet got its name.

Level Two. Explain why we have night and day, and seasons of the year.

Level Three. Write a story for a kindergarten class about the phases of the moon. In your story, explain the phases of the moon using words that a kindergarten class can understand.

Level Four. Draw a model of the solar system showing where the planets are at this time of year in their orbit, and where they will be three months from now.

Level Five. Read about global warming. Make a presentation to the class that explains why global warming might or might not be happening. You may work with a partner and present your report as a debate. Be sure to use facts.

Level Six. Suppose there were a movie about a planet that goes out of orbit and threatens to crash into Earth? Explain why you think this is or is not possible. What would have to happen to make this movie come true?

Brain-Based Learning: Also called *brain-compatible learning*, this is a way of looking at how learning results from the integration of prior knowledge, emotions, physical comfort or discomfort, nutrition, attitude, patterns, frameworks, the arts, interdisciplinary thinking, habits of mind, expectations, and culture. Learning, a human activity, is the result of all that we feel and experience in the learning context. Teachers who are trained in brain-based learning consider how the brain memorizes and retrieves information, how we apply what we learn, and how we can enrich the classroom atmosphere so that the learning is long lasting. A biology teacher who has her students read the literary essays of Lewis Thomas is using brain-based learning theory to reinforce the scientific facts and stimulate an interest in science. She understands that science is more than a collection of facts to be memorized on a test.

Emotions can work for or against effective learning. The student who is nervous about getting it wrong in front of another person may benefit by using computer-assisted learning for remediation. However, we should never minimize the importance of real human contact and expression.

The principles of brain-based learning that play into differentiated instruction are, as extracted from the work of Caine and Caine (1997):

The all-at-once effect. If the brain were a machine, we could call it a parallel processor. This means that we think, emote, imagine, and perceive all at the same time. We are *in the moment.* As teachers, the simultaneity of learning means that students need multisensory input: texts, graphics, video, charts, audio, dialogue, online, and interpersonal interactions to learn complicated material. The more sensory input the learner has, the more likely she is to form connections that will strengthen memory and comprehension.

In addition to these orchestrated learning conditions, the learner is simultaneously affected by stress, hunger, nutrition, lighting, state of comfort, and background noise. While it is true that we can't serve breakfast, control the weather, be personal trainers, tuck kids into bed at a reasonable hour, or chase after kids with a spoonful of cough medicine, we do need to think of teaching as an act of *hospitality*. Like hosts, we invite kids in and make them feel welcome, interesting, and valued. Differentiated instruction means making kids feel that they are *interesting*. Through their own interests, they can learn what we offer. Technology should be viewed not as a replacement for sharing such interests with real live humans in real live time, but as a means to enhance communication and expand interests.

The natural search for meaning. The human brain seeks to make sense, to create order out of chaos. To make sense of things, we categorize, name, connect. We practice the Sesame Street game of "One of These Things Is Not Like the Other." We find sameness and differences. Think about how important this is. It is through discerning similarities and differences that we make meaning out of almost everything we know. We generalize one case to another, find exceptions, figure out where new things belong, define concepts, and apply rules and bend them, all based on how we figure out what is the same and what is different. Data bases, charts, graphs, and tables facilitate the search for meaning and organization.

Pattern-finding. An extension of the *same and different* search for meaning is the brain making meaning by finding patterns, by seeking an organizing principle. A pattern is a repeating and predictable cluster. An organizing principle is a rule that governs how a pattern is put together. Because patterns and clusters are visual, technology helps us create and interpret such relationships.

Emotions and pattern-finding. Not surprisingly, the patterns we discover parallel emotions that we are experiencing. Perhaps we are feeling emotions based on experiences of separation, fear of the unknown, joy, or relief. We may view the world through that lens. To differentiate instruction, we need to show students how to use their emotions to find patterns and make connections. Writing, whether to journalize personal experience or to communicate to a particular audience, is a powerful means of understanding and processing one's emotions; likewise the arts, whether one is creating or receiving artistic expression. By using technology to assist in personal writing and the arts, students can achieve durable learning, according to brain-based theory.

Simultaneous processing of parts and wholes. The best research on reading and writing instruction favors an integrated, differentiated approach, wherein the student learns both the parts (phonics) and the whole (language in context) simultaneously. The brain processes parts and whole simultaneously. This is how musicians and athletes have always learned their crafts: In a practice session, the musician runs scales and sustains tones; then she practices whole pieces. The athlete practices maneuvers, exercises certain muscle groups, and scrimmages. As teachers using technology as a learning tool, we can design tiered tasks that allow students to process and practice discrete parts, as well as whole concepts at varying levels of sophistication.

The role of peripherals. While students are learning the main event, they are also learning from the visuals around them, side conversations and background noise, and other input from the edges of the learning environment. The mind picks up peripheral words and thoughts and brings them to the foreground if they are relevant. This condition of learning supports clusters of computers, where the environment is enriched with productive socialization from peers, teachers, teacher aides, and visuals.

Challenge and threat. Challenge enhances learning; threat inhibits it. We learn best when we feel safe. When threatened, the learner retreats, marshaling energy that would have gone into learning into self-protective defenses. Although we don't want students to sacrifice normal socialization, the computer does offer a certain privacy that reduces the threat of public embarrassment at not knowing an answer or a skill.

Choice Boards: *Choice boards* are charts with pockets to stock task cards. The task cards are arranged in an order that the teacher determines: by skill and readiness levels, by subject, by learning styles or multiple intelligence, by time frames (how long it may take to complete a task). Ideally, choice boards would include tasks involving technology as well as those involving socialization.

Chunking of Information: *Chunking of information* is a term often used to refer to the brain's search for meaningful relationships, patterns, connections. New information needs something to stick to. It must stick to *known* information. We can exploit this brain-fact in how we teach seemingly isolated facts, such as spelling. Some visuals that facilitate chunking of information are graphic organizers, color-coding, Velcro, and magnet boards. Units of information may also be arranged and rearranged physically on a computer screen using Inspiration Software.

Clustering: *Clustering* is a technique of prewriting to formulate groups of related ideas which can later be developed into formal writing. Clustering can also be used as a study technique. It is an effective way of making new information stick to known information. Using clustering as a prewriting/brainstorming technique offers a means of subordinating supportive ideas to key ideas. Inspiration Softwareâ creates cluster diagrams.

Compacting: *Compacting,* also called curriculum compacting, refers to eliminating from the curriculum information and skills that a student has already mastered. Based on a preassessment, the teacher advances students to their instructional level. Compacting is popularly used in math classes. The danger of this pedagogy is that we don't want advanced learners to feel that they are being given more work. Nor do we want some students to feel that they are being sent off on their own. Compacting can work for short periods of time, when students are given choices about what to do with their class time once they have shown mastery on a given topic. In a math class, the teacher may wish to preassess for mastery on rate/time/distance word problems. On determining who already understands the concept, the teacher can have advanced students make up their own word problems based on actual airline schedules, accessing these schedules online. Teachers who use compacting often send letters home to parents explaining the rationale, procedures, and expectations.

Constructivism: Also known as active learning, *constructivism* is the idea that learning is not passively received, but actively constructed by the learner. Differentiated instruction is a constructivist practice. Constructivist practices emphasize use of background knowledge, authentic assessment, metacognition, and use of technology.

Content, Process, and Product: In the language of differentiated instruction promoted by Carol Ann Tomlinson (of the Association for Supervision and Curriculum Development), we often hear these terms. Differentiating content means that students will be learning different information about the same topic. A science class learning about oceanography may differentiate *content* by having four groups of students choose among four topics: measurements, tidal patterns, marine biology, and the ocean floor. Another class may have all of the students learn about ocean measurements by means of whole class instruction, and then differentiate *process* if some students make a color-coded chart, others construct a model, and others make an outline of information from the textbook chapter. To differentiate *product*, students could choose between a written report, an oral report, or a traditional short answer test to show what they know. Technology can be used in all three modes of differentiation.

Cultural Capital: *Cultural capital* refers to the "outside-of-school" self. It includes dialect, socioeconomic status, family attitudes and expectations, exposure to reading material, travel, and sense of safety and well being. Because of the importance of prior knowledge, cultural capital is an extremely important learning factor. Field trips, in-house performances, technology, multi-cultural education, and student exchanges enhances cultural capital build learning capacity. Naturally, students coming from higher socioeconomic backgrounds have access to more sophisticated equipment, and tend to be exposed to more sophisticated language about technology, than their peers who live with fewer material resources. Thus, the achievement gap is very much a gap in access to and experience with technology.

Curriculum Components: The three components of curriculum are information (content), skills, and assessment. Another way of looking at curriculum is: *What concepts and competencies are you learning and how will you show what you know?*

Data-Driven Instruction: *Data-driven instruction* is a term that is used when statistical information forms the basis for educational decisions such as student placement, remediation and enrichment provisions, curriculum changes, grouping, and item analysis on tests.

Deductive Reasoning: *Deductive reasoning* is reasoning that begins with a general rule and then goes into specifics based on that general rule. Direct instruction, where the teacher delivers a body of knowledge, usually depends on deductive reasoning on the part of the students: The teacher gives the generality, such as a spelling rule, and the students apply it to specifics.

Depth and Complexity: When we differentiate instruction for content, we think in terms of how to adjust depth (going into more or less detail in a narrower field) and complexity (having more steps, making more connections, having more interrelated parts. For example, in a social studies class learning about the presidency, *depth* could be achieved by investigating President Roosevelt's relationship to the Supreme Court and the Constitutional issues involved; *complexity* could involve making a graphic representation of the duties of the presidency.

Dialectical Journal: Also called a double-sided journal, the *dialectical journal* is the student's "conversation with herself" regarding a reading. On the left side, the student summarizes the reading. On the right side, she writes affective or interpretative responses. These can include questions, "this reminds me of ..." statements, vocabulary lists, predictions, agree/disagree statements, and further examples. The newspaper or student-selected outside reading works well with the dialectical journal.

Disaggregated Data: *Disaggregated data* are broken down, usually along demographic lines, including girls and boys, economic need, income level, English proficiency, learning disabilities, ethnicity, region, and other local concerns, such as which students took which preparatory courses, had which teachers, were in which programs, and so forth. Disaggregated data show us how various subgroups perform.

E-Communications: E-communications include electronic communication modes such as e-mail, e-conferencing, message-boarding, threaded discussions, list servers, and other interactives.

Emotional Intelligence: *Emotional intelligence* refers to a person's ability to function well in social situations, especially stress-producing ones. Emotional intelligence involves communication skills, self-control, perceptiveness to the needs and concerns of others, self-understanding, and intuition. Timing, humor, empathy, and patience are characteristics of emotional intelligence. Because cooperative learning projects require emotional intelligence, social skills must be part of the learning process, expectations, and rubrics. These social skills involve leadership and working under the direction of a leader, sharing the work and the credit, subordinating personal needs, listening, and compromising.

Embedded Application: *Embedded application* occurs when a skill, such as recording measurements, is an integral part of a learning task, such as writing a lab report or completing a WebQuest.

Entry Points: The term *entry points* comes from Howard Gardner's work on multiple intelligence. Gardner (1991, p. 93) names five entry points, or pathways, to learning a given topic.

These are narrational (entering the topic via a story), logical/quantitative (entering the topic via numbers, deductive reasoning, or scientific inquiry), foundational (entering the topic via its philosophy or key words), aesthetic (entering the topic via the arts), and experiential (entering the topic via physical contact by manipulating the objects and materials involved).

Features of Differentiation: Differentiated instruction can be about any or all of the following: *pacing, degree of structure that the teacher provides, degree of independence of the learner, number of facets in the learning task, level of abstractness or concreteness, and level of depth and complexity.*

Flexible Grouping: *Flexible grouping* is a key practice of differentiating instruction. Groups can be formed in various ways: interest, self-selection, or random. What we *don't* want is the formation of groups that are obviously ability-based. Such grouping is humiliating to the low functioning group and breeds arrogance and a sense of entitlement in the so-called smart group. Cooperative learning groups work best when roles are clearly assigned. One popular method is based on *literature circles*. In a literature circle, each member of the group has a job to do: word looker-upper, metaphor finder, illustrator, title maker, and connectors.

Graphic Organizer: A graphic organizer, also called a concept map or web, is any kind of diagram or outline which helps the learner to arrange information visually. The Harvard outline and the sentence diagram are graphic organizers which have been around for more than a hundred years to help learners. The trouble is the graphic organizer can become so complicated that it becomes its own taskmaster. Popular graphic organizers are the Venn diagram for comparison/contrast, the Frayer model for concept attainment, the KWL chart for reading comprehension, and the flow chart for sequential information. Power Point and Inspiration Software produce excellent graphic organizers.

Inclusion Classes: Often called *collaboration classes*, inclusion classes are based on the model in which students with special needs are taught within the regular class, along with a special education teacher who works collaboratively with the subject area teacher. There are various models of inclusion. Sometimes, the special education teacher is present for every class; other times, she may work with mainstream classes in two subject areas, alternating from one to the other. Sometimes, the special education teacher and her class work as a separate class most of the time, merging with the mainstream classes for appropriate projects. For collaboration to work, teachers need training, common planning time, opportunity for reflective practice and lots of communication and administrative support.

Inductive Reasoning: *Inductive reasoning* is reasoning that begins with the specifics and draws generalities based on them. A detective gathering information about a crime uses inductive reasoning to draw a conclusion about what happened.

Inquiry Activities: Reading specialists refer to such activities as the KWL chart (see the next entry in this chapter) as an inquiry activity. The reader establishes overt goals for the reading, sets up expectations, makes predictions, and self-monitors her reading, aware of what she is looking for in the text.

KWL Chart: The popular and effective three-column *KWL chart* stands for *know, want to know, learned*. Here's how it works: Before reading, the student jots down what she already knows about the subject. In the second column, she writes what she wants to know. After the reading, in the third column, she writes what she's learned. This marshals prior knowledge and focuses the reading. The KWL comports with everything we know about effective reading. It should be used in every class.

Learning Centers: *Learning centers* are usually associated with elementary classrooms, but it's possible to have them in a middle school class. With learning centers, the room is physically arranged so that students interested in a particular type of learning can congregate. Centers can be oriented around activities, readings, topics, or themes. Learning centers work well with contracts. In a seventh-grade social studies class learning about ancient Greece, students turned the classroom into a museum. The groups created stations based on philosophy, government, theater, and architecture. Each station had student-designed activities, which the class completed by rotating around the room.

Learning Contracts: *Learning contracts* are written agreements between teacher and student stipulating that certain learning tasks will be carried out by a certain time. A contract is a *negotiated agreement* between two sides. When a teacher hands out an assignment and declares that it is due by her deadline, it is *not* a learning contract. The student must have a part in drawing up the terms of the contract. In a creative writing class, the teacher and the student could discuss the nature of the writing project (making a short story out of a poem), the length, interim due dates, and criteria for evaluation.

Learning Logs: A *learning log* is a general term for some sort of tracking system in which the learner will record her own learning. Entries can include questions, predictions, graphic organizers, summaries, mnemonic devices, connections to real life and other subject areas, diagrams, and vocabulary lists. KWL charts and dialectical journals are often part of the learning log. Because learning logs are often in the form of a list or chart, tables are a useful visual for them.

Learning Style: A person's *learning style* is her best way of processing, remembering, and using information. We usually think of learning style in terms of the senses: visual learners, auditory learners, and kinesthetic learners. Some people learn best by socializing; others by writing; others by talking to themselves aloud. We speak of brain laterality: The right hemisphere is the realm of intuitive learning; the left, of quantitative learning. Special education teachers are the experts in adapting information to a student's best learning style. Effective learners have a keen understanding of their own learning styles.

Technology plays well into learning styles because of its visual, interactive, and communicative applications.

Microskills and Macroskills: Microskills are skills in isolation, such as the skill of arranging things in order. Macroskills are microskills used in combination. Problem solving calls for macroskills.

Multiple Intelligence Theory: Developed by Howard Gardner, the *multiple intelligence theory* posits that there are eight different kinds of intelligence. These are verbal-linguistic, musical-rhythmic, logical-mathematical, interpersonal, intrapersonal (knowing of the self), bodily-kinesthetic, visual-spatial, and naturalistic (understanding the natural world). Multiple intelligence theory plays an important role in differentiated instruction.

Portfolios: *Portfolios* are organized collections of evidence of learning over time. There are all different types of portfolios. A portfolio differs from a folder with papers stuffed in it in that a portfolio represents a carefully selected array of work samples which show goals, growth, and introspection. Portfolios are just as valid whether they represent an entire school year, or one particular area of study. They are an excellent way of differentiating instruction and are limited only by your imagination.

Scaffolding: As the metaphor implies, *scaffolding* is a support system for learning. The purpose of a scaffold device is to allow the learner to build new information on a foundation of prior knowledge. Scaffolds can be graphic organizers, short answer questions, dialogue, word banks, and other learning supports. The social studies teacher whose students are writing a document-based essay based on a collection of Matthew Brady Civil War photographs has students answer guided questions about each photograph. The students will then use their information to compose the essay.

Schema: A *schema* is an organizational framework of knowledge on which new knowledge can be built. Having a schema allows us to mentally fill in details and make assumptions about whatever it is that we are learning. The more sophisticated the learner, the more elaborate is the schema that she brings to the body of knowledge being learned. We hear a lot about schemas in differentiated instruction pedagogy. This is because any student's ability to learn new information will be based on the richness of the schema that they bring to the subject. Assessing the detail and accuracy of a student's schema for a particular topic is one way of preassessing.

Semantic Maps: Semantic maps are graphic representations of vocabulary. One kind of semantic map is the *yes/no/maybe model* in which the student writes the name of a concept, such as *civilizations*, at the head of the paper. She then sorts various words in the yes/no/maybe columns, depending on whether they are civilizations, not civilizations, or ambiguities. Other forms of semantic maps show related words, etymology trees, synonym/antonym lists, characteristics or elements of the concept, and the like. The value of the semantic map is that it calls for critical thinking about what a concept name really means.

Show What You Know Assessments: *Show what you know* assessments are demonstrations of the student's knowledge in a form that is chosen by the student. The student makes a proposal, describing how her project will display her knowledge. She may offer to make up a short answer or essay test, make an oral or written report, or do a creative project. One caveat: The product cannot be something that can be taken in whole from another source. It should have enough of an in-class component that the teacher sees the product being constructed.

Socratic Seminar: A *Socratic seminar* is a student-centered, open-ended discussion based on a text. The text may be print or nonprint. The purpose of Socratic seminar is to invite conversation that is grounded in textual information. A Socratic seminar does not end in closure because its purpose is to stimulate independent thought rather than to come to any particular conclusion. The teacher's role in a Socratic seminar is to ask questions and direct the students to focus on the text for their answers.

Textual Features: Textual features are the visual cues that assist reading comprehension, especially in textbooks. Textual features that are helpful to the reading process are writing in columns, pictures, graphics, headings, bold-faced and italic type, introductory and chapter-end questions. Textual features help the reader scan for specific information, and direct the reader's attention to key points.

Threaded Discussions: *Threaded discussions* are ongoing e-conversations on a certain topic. Teachers can monitor, direct, and assess threaded discussions based on academic topics.

Tiered Tasks: *Tiered* assignments, usually presented on three levels, are tasks which are constructed with different levels of depth and complexity in mind. Some teachers use preassessment to determine which students are best suited to which tier. Others rely on student choice.

Think-Pair-Share: *Think-pair-share* is a cooperative learning strategy in which students are given a question and then asked to think about the answer, discuss their thoughts briefly with a partner, and then share the fruits of their discussion with others.

Transcendent Thinking Modes: *Transcendent thinking modes* are ways of thinking that go beyond the obvious: comparison/contrast, cause/effect, finding relationships and making connections, metaphorical thinking.

Unit Menus: *Unit menus* are lists of tasks that students can choose from. They differ from tiered tasks because, in a unit menu, the tasks are not leveled by degrees of sophistication. Unit menu choices often represent various learning styles. Items on the unit menu should take most students approximately the same time to complete.

Web-Hosting Sites: Web sites, such as myschoolonline.com and filamentality.com, are *Web-hosting sites*, through which you can set up your own Web site, using their templates.

WebQuests: *WebQuests* are research projects in which the information can be found on various sites on the Web. The student begins with a question (not just a topic) and produces a multi-faceted answer. The answer can be expressed as a PowerPoint presentation, a documented written report, a creative writing piece, a three-dimensional construction, a skit, or anything else that shows understanding.

Whole-Part-Whole: *Whole-part-whole* is a brain-compatible perspective on learning which suggests that we go from the generality to the specifics and then back to the generality.

3
Tiered Tasks

Tiered tasking is a mainstay in differentiated instruction. A tiered task structure typically presents three levels, graduating in depth and complexity, which offer opportunities to actively learn the same concept. Tiered tasks should differ in quality, not just quantity.

I'll say at the outset that I am not in favor of teacher-imposed ability grouping. In my opinion, students at the secondary level should be allowed to choose their level, and be graded accordingly.

Tiered tasks differ from unit menus. Unit menus, described in Chapter 4, offer a wider array of choices, and the choices are not necessarily more sophisticated than one another. In a unit menu, the choices are based on a student's preference. A tiered task structure is usually tri-leveled, and the levels are definitely based on graduated degrees of sophistication. However, in a well-designed tiered-task structure, each student should be expending comparable amounts of time on their task.

As with unit menus and WebQuests, you can find ready-made tiered tasks in books and on the Internet. And as with unit menus and WebQuests, you may prefer to design your own tasks, maintaining control of the learning experience. If you have the time, it's probably better to design these yourself, as you have your own students in mind as you do so. Once you have a template for a good tiered task, you will find them easier to construct.

In a tiered task, process and assessment overlap: Students produce something that uses content in a certain way. A tiered task is a performance of some kind: a written piece, a presentation or demonstration, a collection, or an exhibit. Designing a tiered task is an opportunity to think creatively about teaching. You will need to consider three strands:

1. **Structure**: time and resource management

2. **Philosophy**: grading and grouping

3. **Process**: writing directions for three tasks appropriate to your class and content

Like most complexities, the design of a tiered task is recursive: You start with a draft that you will refine as you work out the details. Rich Santana teaches middle school social studies. His topic is the functioning of the Articles of Confederation and how this document gave way to the Constitution. Rich wants students to understand conceptual differences between loosely confederated states and the federal system, as well as how individuals are affected in their daily lives by the system of government that organizes their society.

Rich needs to impart information to the whole class, to build the knowledge base that the tiered tasks will advance. (Usually, tiered tasks are the way in which students construct and internalize knowledge given to the whole class.) Rich may be explaining content through a *whole-class* lesson, requiring students to take notes; he may be assigning pages in the textbook, scaffolding the reading with some chapter questions; he may be showing a video. In any case, Rich's students will go into the tiered tasks knowing, but not really understanding, the nature of the Articles of Confederation and the Constitution.

Consider the status of knowledge at the point at which students face the tiered tasks: They have new knowledge, but not understanding. The understanding will come through process, as they put their information to work to meet the requirements of the tiered task. Thus, the tiered task becomes both process learning and a product to be assessed.

I rely on the phrase *To better understand...*, when I construct tiered tasks:

♦ "To better understand how the Puritans lived in the New World..."

♦ "To better understand igneous rock formation..."

♦ "To better understand how an artist's physical environment affects his or her work..."

♦ "To better understand how meter affects meaning in poetry. . ."

♦ "To better understand the Pythagorean theorem..."

To create effective tiered tasks, you have to first ascertain whether or not your students have a basic understanding of this concept: Tiered tasking is not about learning something for the first time. It's about going beyond the basic knowledge, to extent that one can, to solidify and advance that knowledge. Tiered tasking, then, is a secondary step in the learning process, the first step being the whole-class instruction that lays out the foundations and the language of the topic.

Planning the Tiered Task

Structure: Time and Resource Management

Rich needs to allocate class time for whole-class instruction, homework (reading from the text and a follow-up quiz), explaining the tasks, having the students do the work, and having them share their results. Theoretically, the tasks should demand comparable amounts of time, but some students will finish early; others will need more time. (Some will finish early only because they rushed to get it done, and did so carelessly; some will need more time only because they misused their allocated class time. Rich needs to redirect off-task behaviors by having checkpoints and consequences for failing to meet them because of off-task behaviors.)

Even an experienced teacher will misjudge how long new tasks will take to complete. Rich is ready to provide supplemental learning, such as portfolio work or outside readings. He also has a video about the Constitutional convention that early finishers can watch in the media center. They can earn bonus points by taking a quick quiz following the video.

Rich meets with his resource people, the library media specialist and computer lab coordinator. He will provide them with a copy of the tiers and a simple sign-off sheet, to indicate whether students have been excessively unproductive. He will describe what his students should look like (working in pairs, working in groups, working independently) doing their work, and what they should be able to show when they claim to be finished.

Philosophy: Grading and Grouping

When I give workshops to teachers on tiered tasking, two concerns arise. The first is grading. Some teachers feel strongly that students should be given opportunities to do the best they can and should be graded based on their own abilities. "Since everyone does not possess equal ability, it is perfectly fair to grade students based on their own abilities, comparing them only to themselves." These teachers favor having all students eligible to receive top grades, regardless of the relative sophistication of the three tasks. Other teachers insist that product be evaluated on quality alone, independent of the assumed level of ability of the student. "To grade students based on an assumed level of ability is condescending," they say. These teachers hold that a task which is on the lower end of depth and complexity should not be considered of the same merit as a higher-level task. They might put limits, known as *ceilings*, on the maximum grade that the lower tasks could be eligible to receive. Such ceilings are the embodiment, and another incarnation, of weighted grades. Call it what you will.

Who will do which task? Will students self-select, or will they do the task that the teacher assigns? If the former, what if they select unwisely? If the latter, what if they choose the easy way? And what if the teacher's judgment is mistaken? It stands to reason that teachers who favor subjective grades tend to favor assigning students to particular tasks. After all, if you allow students to self-select in a system where an A is an A regardless of what you chose to do, how many students are going to opt for the most challenging task on the list? Therefore, teachers who favor subjectivity in grading usually want to assign students to particular tasks, based on what the teacher believes is at the level of each student. The teacher's belief can be informed by various kinds of facts, figures, and perceptions.

It generally falls out that middle school teachers lean toward subjective assessment; and high school teachers, toward objective. It should also be noted that high school students (and their parents) are usually more concerned about grade point averages, class rank, placement, and formal academic recognition than are middle school students, for obvious reasons. So goes the natural tension between high school and middle school teachers.

Discussions of these issues become heated, but the fact is that in traditional classrooms, less able students obviously don't receive top level grades anyway. Tasks and tests that challenge the most capable students simply defeat those who need more scaffolding, more concretions, and more reinforcement of the fundamentals. If their grades were stellar, they wouldn't need the lower level tasks anyway. As for capable students opting for tasks that are beneath their instructional level, they can always choose to undersell themselves by doing just enough to get by, or even less, in traditional situations. When we put emotions, assumptions, and frustrations aside, we're left with some students outmatched by certain academic demands while others skate by in a self-selected state of blissful *unchallengement*. Nevertheless, I have found, to my chagrin, that training in differentiated instruction can run aground on the rocks of the subjectivity/objectivity debate.

So, then, the second strand of planning a tiered task is philosophical. Are you going to weight the grades, or will everyone be eligible for the same grades? Will students choose their own tiers, or will you assign them? If the latter, will your decisions be informed by appropriate data? If so, will there be controversy? Will objections to your grading system come from parents? Students? Administration? Colleagues? How will you answer each of these constituents? Take into consideration the grading philosophy of your school. Be armed with justifications for your decisions. Be consistent. Be sure that everyone knows the rules in advance and that they are presented in a clear, written form.

Here are several alternatives to the grading problem. You don't have to select one and stick with it for the whole year. Perhaps the best way to really establish fairness and equity is to use a combination of these models:

♦ *Equity (teacher-selected tiers).* You assign the tasks, based on explainable criteria, such as performance on a recent test. All students are eligible to receive top grades if they perform to the specifications of the task.

♦ *Ranges.* Students self-select, with the understanding that only the top tier carries a maximum grade of 100. The lower tiers can be maxed out at 85 and 75.

♦ *Rubrics.* You can design the same rubric for all three tasks, permitting any student to receive a top score if he or she shows higher level thinking on the rubric. This system has a lot of advantages; the disadvantage is that it is possible that your lower level tiers will not show higher level thinking because higher level thinking is not requested. For example, the student may be asked to recall and summarize the key points of the Articles of Confederation. Although such a task may be perfectly appropriate and challenging for some students, it not higher level thinking, and so can't make it to the upper end of the rubric.

♦ *Bonus Points.* Here, you give students additional ways to earn extra points by doing higher level thinking over and above the tier that you assigned them. The disadvantage is that not only is this more work for you, but you're in for unpleasantness if the student's extra work falls short of the higher level thinking necessary to earn the extra points. If a student is not ready to handle the Articles of Confederation beyond a literal level, she's likely to hand you a summary when you asked for analysis, leaving you back where you started, but with a disgruntled student who feels that she did something for nothing.

♦ *Combinations.* You can plan for a certain number of tiered tasks per quarter, say four. Tier 3s are worth up to 50 points each; tier 2s, 33 points; 3s, 25 points. This way, everyone is eligible to receive the maximum of points. This is a satisfying compromise, but you'll need to be extra organized. Color coding the tiers might help.

Constructing the Tiers

Constructing the tiers is the fun part. I'm going to show you two systems for building on depth and complexity to design your tiers. The first is the famous Bloom's hierarchy of thinking. The second is S. I. Hayakawa's abstraction ladder.

Before we do that, you need to know where you're going. Coming back to our example of the Articles of Confederation, Rich can express his central concept as a behavioral objective: "Students will be able to articulate the differences between the Articles of Confederation and the Constitution, and how the former led to the latter." Or, he can express the central concept as a statement: "The Articles of Confederation created problems which were eventually solved, after much debate, by the replacement of the Articles with the United States Constitution."

We need to avoid assigning any tasks that can be fetched intact from the Internet. Charts that compare the Articles to the Constitution can be easily found, as can paragraphs from textbooks giving that same information. We want more than copying, so we have to think creatively about how student can embed the information into some kind of constructed response.

Organizing Principles of Tiered Tasking

Tiered tasks can be organized according to a variety of learning principles. What follows are examples of tiered tasks organized by the following principles:

- Bloom's taxonomy
- Going from concrete go abstract thinking
- Decreasing support (scaffolding)
- Increasing depth (more details on the same exemplar)
- Increasing complexity (more steps, more connections to related subjects)
- Organization: classifying, categorizing

Tiered tasks can be organized around Bloom's taxonomy (shortened to Bloom) (Benjamin, 2002). When educators say "Bloom," they are referring to six levels of learning, from most basic (knowledge) to most sophisticated (evaluation). Bloom's taxonomy establishes this hierarchy:

1. *Knowledge.* The learner has the information. She knows the principles of the Articles of Confederation and those of the United States Constitution.

2. *Comprehension.* The learner understands the information. She can explain how the Articles form organizing principles as to how states operate and how the federal government operates, and how the Constitution does so as well.

   A performance task at the level of knowledge/comprehension might have the students express key points of the Articles and the Constitution in their own words. Or, given wording by either document, the student could tell to which document that wording belongs. Or, the student can identify wording or concepts that are not included in either document.

3. *Application.* The learner can use the information. Given a problem, she can determine whether that problem falls under the realm of the state or the federal government.

4. *Analysis.* The learner can take apart the information and put it back together, with an understanding of the part-whole relationship.

Given the statement, "The Constitution gives more power to the Federal government than did the Articles," the student can cite proof.

A performance task at the level of application/analysis might have the students explain to a petitioner that a particular suit falls or does not fall within the realm of the federal government, and why this is so, referring to the relevant clauses in the documents.

5. *Synthesis.* The learner can bring together disparate information, revising their concepts of reality as new information reshapes the known. A student thinking at this level can determine whether or not a "what if?" scenario fits into the parameters set by the Articles or the Constitution.

6. *Evaluation.* The learner can make judgments based on criteria. Comparison/contrast is part of evaluation, because it involves implicit criteria. The student who can think of the Articles and Constitution at this high level would be able to determine which system offers the most personal liberty, how these systems compare to other compacts, and the extent to which either document conforms to the principles set forth by the founders.

A performance task at the level of synthesis/evaluation might have students compare how the Articles would have determined the outcome of a contemporary social problem.

Example of Tiered Task Structured by Bloom's Taxonomy

Rich chose PowerPoint as the vehicle through which his students would express their understanding of the differences between the Articles and the Constitution. PowerPoint offers an efficient framework for expressing comparisons: colors, shapes, and columns. Also, the bulleted format allows the learner to show point-by-point comparisons.

Whole-Class Foundations: Rich gave his students a one-page chart showing how the Articles and the Constitution compared on 11 key points.

Directions to the Students: (Draft)

Tier One (Reinforcing the Foundations): Students choosing this tier will demonstrate knowledge of the difference between the Articles and the Constitution by constructing complete sentences based on the information given on each line of the chart. For each line of information, use a conjunction such as "but," or "however."

Tier Two (Building on the Foundations): Students choosing this tier will apply and analyze the differences between the Articles and the Constitution by giving a hypothetical example of several of the boxes on the chart.

Tier Three (Transcending the Foundations): Students choosing this tier will synthesize and evaluate by showing how three contemporary problems (social, economic, and international) would have been handled by the Articles and the Constitution, respectively.

Looking over this draft, Rich thought that although the tasks were on point for the three levels of learning, the wording of the tasks was uninviting. This is when Rich decided to incorporate PowerPoint, to enliven the tasks and make them visual.

Directions to the Students (Revisions):

Tier One (Reinforcing the Foundations): Using two colors as backgrounds in your PowerPoint presentation, make a series of slides that shows the difference between the Articles and the Constitution. Write complete sentences for each slide. For each sentence, underline the key phrase. Your sentences should begin with the words, "Under the Articles of Confederation…" or "Under the United States Constitution…" In your last slide, write a clear statement explaining why the federalists favored the Constitution over the Articles.

Tier Two (Building on the Foundations): Make a PowerPoint presentation that shows the eleven key points of difference between the Articles and Constitution. Represent one key point, with both the Articles and the Constitution, on each slide (eleven slides). Then, make five slides with "If… then…" statements showing what Alexander Hamilton and the federalists considered as disadvantages of the Articles.

Tier Three (Transcending the Foundations): Make a PowerPoint presentation that introduces each of the 11 key points of difference with an example of a contemporary problem that would be solved either at the state level or the federal level under the Articles and under the Constitution. Choose one contemporary social problem, one economic problem, and one international relations problem.

Hand in your PowerPoint presentations on a disk or e-mail them to the class Web site.

You may find this list of "tasking verbs" helpful as you design tiers based on Bloom's taxonomy:

Tier One: (knowledge and comprehension)

List, enumerate, retell, rephrase, arrange, organize, outline, show, locate

Tier Two: (application and analysis)

Solve, explain, interpret, apply, analyze (take apart and put back together), generalize, draw conclusions

Tier Three: (synthesis and evaluation)

Create, devise, propose, defend, oppose, debate, argue, judge

I have not included some key tasking verbs here, such as *summarize, compare and contrast, and respond.* I left these out because these are the kinds of verbs that may be at any of the levels, depending on the sophistication of the subject matter, as well as the amount of scaffolding provided. English teachers view summary as a lower level skill, a skill that we work hard to move beyond. However, if the language is dense with abstractions, allusions, complicated sentences, and sophisticated assumptions about the reader, then summary becomes a more elevated skill.

Comparing and contrasting can be a lower level skill if students are working directly from a chart in which the points of difference are already presented. In such cases, students are merely taking information and putting it in another form. This is a knowledge and comprehension level of thinking. However, comparing and contrasting can be an extremely high level skill if students have to make fine distinctions between like things, or, conversely, if they are perceiving connections between seemingly disparate things. So, comparison/contrast tasks can appear on all three levels, depending on how much the student has to do original thinking.

Responses such as annotating text, note taking, and dialectical journaling can all be high level if the student is producing evidence of transcendent thinking. But they are lower level if the student is making meaning by restating text or lecture which is already organized and relatively accessible. (This is not to denigrate the value of having students annotate, take notes, and write dialectical journals. These responses are valuable ways to construct and remember information.)

Let me make the point that you can tier on the basis of *one* of these verbs. Doing so would be differentiating content. For example, suppose you wanted to teach students the skill of summary (or paraphrase). You could put your most able readers on a poem with a lot of allusions, or with inverted syntax, while your grade-level and struggling readers are summarizing (or paraphrasing) more accessible text.

Concrete to Abstract

Another organizing principle for tiered tasking is going from the concrete to the abstract. The more abstract you ask students to get, the more sophisticated is the task. The extent to which something is concrete is the extent to which we conjure up the same image when the thing is mentioned. That is, we have the same referent. As we go up the ladder of abstraction, we are less and less likely to conjure the same visual image (referent) for the subject.

We make theories accessible to novices by translating theories into concretions. For example, in math, if you were to teach the concept of probability using only theories and abstractions, you'd be losing a lot of students. But if you were to teach probability by using the concrete example of pulling matching socks and underwear out of the dresser drawers, you'd have a better chance of communicating.

Tiering Math Tasks by Teaching with Concrete Examples

Math is a subject of abstracts. To understand these abstract concepts, many students need to form mental pictures of concrete images. Most of us, when we first learned the concept of fractions, were given the mental picture of a pie: We could easily visualize half a pie, half of half a pie, and so forth. Mathematically adept students may be comfortable with abstracts, or, they may be mathematically adept because they are able to transit from abstract concepts to mental pictures and then back again to the abstract. When teaching a mixed class, the math teacher needs a good storehouse of concrete images to correspond with abstract concepts.

In his book, *Math for Humans: Teaching Math Through 8 Intelligences*, Mark Wahl (1999) presents copious models to help students understand the relationship between the abstract and the concrete. Some of these are described in next section.

Models for Tiering Math Tasks by Going from Concrete to Abstract

Whole Number Characteristics and The Incredible Number Detection Machine

Overview: This task is the construction of a binary system that sorts whole numbers by their characteristics. It is a flow chart, but the students will construct this flow chart to resemble machinery: a system of pipes, funnels, branches, joints, and so forth. The Incredible Number Detection Machine can be created through PowerPoint, word processing, Inspiration Software or other applications that create and organize shapes and directional signals.

Whole-Class Foundations: The teacher explains what she means by number characteristics. Various characteristics can be considered, such as odd, even, prime, divisibility, and more sophisticated characteristics such as squares and cubes. She then explains how flow charts work to track, sort, classify, and ultimately detect (find out) targeted information.

To concretize the concept of detection, Mark Wahl suggests that you get students thinking about other kinds of detectors, such as metal detectors, smoke detectors, a police detective, and so forth. What do these detectors do to determine whether a given characteristic is present?

The teacher then shows simple examples of how a flow chart can detect the presence of a given number, by passing that number through a binary system: Is the number divisible by 7? Is it greater than or less than 11? Is the number odd?

In the tiered task presented here, students at all three tiers are working with the same range of whole numbers, 1–16.

Tier Three: (most abstract)

Sort every whole number in the set of (1–16) by divisibility. Express, in mathematical terms, the characteristics of these whole numbers. If you need assistance, you may refer to Tier Two and Tier Three.

Tier Two: (less concrete, more abstract)

Draw a flow chart that paths every whole number in the set of (1–16) by divisibility by 7, 5, and 3. In your flow chart, draw the paths that each number in the set would go to, depending on its divisibility by 7, 5, and 3. Make your flow chart resemble a machine. Your Incredible Number Machine should have three kinds of parts: Mixers (marked with questions or operations), Pipes (Y or N paths) and Terminators (your numbers).

Tier One: (most concrete)

You have been given an empty Incredible Number Detector Machine. Your job is to insert the proper questions or operations that will lead to the detection of the whole numbers 1–16. Your questions must be yes/no questions. You may ask "greater than/less than" questions. You may ask questions about the number of digits and if the digits are the same. You may ask questions about whether the number is odd or even.

Your operations may be division, multiplication, addition, or subtraction.

Your machine consists of Mixers, Pipes, and Terminators. The Mixers are labeled with questions or operations. The Pipes are marked Y or N. The Pipes lead to other Mixers or to Terminators. When you get to a Terminator, you have detected your number.

Cartesian Coordinates and Ruby Rock

Overview: Using the system of longitude and latitude on a map, the teacher presents a problem that is solvable through plotting Cartesian coordinates.

Whole-class Foundations: Some entry points to Cartesian coordinates are locations on a street map and the game *Battleship*.

Tier Three (most abstract): Locate 15 degrees East, 15 degrees North on the X and Y axes.

Tier Two (more abstract, less concrete): Using a world map, locate and name the coordinates of the city Zinder in eastern Africa.

Tier One (most concrete): Think of yourself as an adventurer, flying a small plane over the savannah of eastern Africa. When you land in the savannah, there are no landmarks in sight. You spy a huge gem—a ruby that surely is of inestimable value. However, the ruby is embedded in an iron outcropping. You'll need to free it with some tools that you left back at the travel agency. Trouble is, how can you locate this remarkable gem again when you return? You don't want to draw any attention to your priceless find by planting a flag or setting up flares.

To solve your problem, you will need to think of the Earth as a piece of graph paper. The ruby has an address, a location marked by latitude and longitude lines. By knowing your coordinates, your navigation team can use the Global Positioning Satellite system can pinpoint the ruby's location so that you can find it again. (They'll want a piece of the action.)

Other Models That Concretize Math

1. Abstract Concept

Patterns can be expressed in mathematical terms, as can variations and changes in patterns.

Concrete expression of this abstract concept:

Household textile patterns: quilts, wallpaper, china

What are the symbols?

How are the symbols put together to form a pattern?

Is the pattern based on multiplication or addition?

What are the multiples of the pattern?

Does the pattern have sub-patterns?

2. Abstract Concept

When a transversal intersects two parallel lines, pairs of alternate interior angles appear to be congruent.

Concrete expression of this abstract concept:

When we look at the zigzag patterns of exterior stairwells, such as fire escapes, we see that the stairs form the transversal that intersects the parallel lines which are the landings.

3. Abstract Concept

Quadratic equations are graphed as parabolas.

Concrete expression of this abstract concept: Think of baseball. When the batter hits the ball, it travels along a path called its trajectory. A trajectory is the path that an object travels once put into motion. The trajectory forms a parabola.

4. Abstract Concept

Ratios of measures of corresponding sides are equivalent.

Concrete expression of this abstract concept: When a photographer enlarges a print, the enlargement must bear the same horizontal/vertical ratio as the original print for the photograph to look the same. This principle also applies to the formatting notice that introduces home video versions of movies: "This film has been formatted to fit your screen." The ratio has been changed from the "envelope" form of a movie screen to the "box" form of your television screen.

5. Abstract Concept

The counting principle posits that if Activity A can occur in any of m ways and Activity B can occur in any of n ways, then the total number of ways both activities can occur is given by the product mn.

Concrete expression of this abstract concept: Use familiar life experiences involving variables, such as wardrobe choices, choices of entrees and side dishes, socks pulled out of the sock drawer, candy choices, and so forth.

6. Abstract Concept

To compute the permutations of four factors, use the counting principle.

Concrete expression of this abstract concept: Use letter blocks to show how many different ways four letters can come together to spell a given four letter word.

7. Abstract Concept

If three sides of one triangle are congruent to the corresponding parts of another triangle, then the triangles are congruent.

Concrete expression of this abstract concept: You can easily understand this axiom by constructing (drawing or building) congruent triangles of varying sizes.

It may be easy for math teachers to assume that concepts familiar to them are concrete, when in fact they are abstract. Remember that a concept is abstract if everyone does not conjure up the same mental picture of it. Symbols are abstract. Pictures are concrete. Sometimes math teachers teach the abstract concept and then assess the knowledge by giving a concrete application, a word problem. Students often find this transition extremely difficult. That is because they don't fully understand the abstraction to begin with. They may have memorized it, they may be able to perform mechanically on a series of "examples" that vary a particular theme, but they can't transit from the abstract to the concrete. They can't *apply*. A sounder teaching practice is to work in the opposite direction: present the concrete first, and then move to the abstraction. Offer opportunities and reminders to students to concretize and visualize as they learn math. This habit of visualization is essential to reading comprehension as well.

Summary

When we tier tasks in math, Tier One should be grounded in the concrete, allowing the student to visualize real objects in a real context. Tier Two should allow the student to transit from the visual to the symbolic (concrete to abstract) in the process of solving the problem. Tier Three should be at the abstract level. Standardized math tests require that the student function at the abstract level. However, students need to develop the habit of mind to transit from abstract to concrete, and then back to abstract.

This example is given to a ninth-grade English class. Students are studying *Romeo and Juliet*.

The Learning Context

Ellin Worley shows her ninth-grade classes a 42-minute video called "Shakespeare in the Classroom" by Miramax. This video uses excerpts from Tom Stoppard's "Shakespeare in Love" to introduce students to the world of Shakespeare and to *Romeo and Juliet* in particular.

Targeted Concept and Tiered Structure

Ellin wants her students to understand the extent to which financial interests shaped the theatre in Shakespeare's day, as portrayed in *Shakespeare in Love*. She has organized the three tiers by their graduating levels of complexity.

Tiered Task: *Shakespeare in Business: Money Makes the Globe Go Round*

How are the characters in the film portrayed as being controlled by, and controlling others by, money?

Tier Three: The Influence Pyramid

Using Inspiration Software—make a pyramid with a five-block base. On the top of the pyramid, write the name of a character who influences others by his or her money. In the block below the base, show how that character influences two other characters; then, the three characters beneath them on the pyramid, and so on until you've reached the base of five blocks.

Tier Two: The Influence Web

Using PowerPoint, make a web (interconnected lines) showing the influence of money on six characters. Write examples along the lines. Use arrows to show where the money is going.

Tier One: The Influence Chart

Using the table format in Microsoft Word, make a character chart that includes Queen Elizabeth, Lord Wessex, Viola, Master Will, Ned Allen, Mr. Henning, and one other of your choice. Label two rows as "influences others" and "is influenced by." In the squares, give specific examples of how money is an influence. You may express yourself in phrases or in sentences.

Checklist for Evaluating Your Tiered Tasks:

- ◆ Are all students working toward a unified concept that requires higher level thinking?
- ◆ Can you expect all of the tasks to require approximately the same amount of time to complete?
- ◆ Are the tasks worded in a clear manner?
- ◆ Does each task meet your learning objectives?
- ◆ If the tasks use technology, does the technology support the learning, or is it a distraction?
- ◆ If you are assigning students to a task, do you have data to support your decision?
- ◆ If students are self-selecting, do you have incentives for selecting the more challenging tasks?
- ◆ Are students clear on how these tasks will be evaluated?
- ◆ Have you made plans for early finishers and those who need additional time?
- ◆ Are the tasks worded in an inviting, encouraging manner?
- ◆ Are tasks leveled by sound learning principles?

Preassessing for Tiered Tasking

If you are making decisions about where to place students on the task list, then you need data to support your decisions. Such data can be as close by as the most recent performance task or test. Based on that vehicle, you decide who needs to reinforce the basics before moving on, and who is ready for advancement. If you have given a traditional short answer test, chart results with a bar graph out of Excel. If you have given a subjective test, such as an essay or other performance task, you might divide students up in accordance to their neediest areas on your rubric.

Let's say that you teach social studies. Your students have completed the performance task of analyzing a political cartoon for context and purpose. Your rubric specifies that the students need to show a clear and complete understanding of the following implications of the political cartoon:

- ◆ Subject
- ◆ Occasion
- ◆ Audience
- ◆ Purpose
- ◆ Speaker

As you go through the work, flag one or two of the neediest areas. Students who have aced the task can move on to contemporary cartoons (or historical ones), or can try creating their own, using Clip Art. Remediation for the others can provide scaffolding questions for the targeted field.

Your assessment of the responses to the political cartoons may inform you that students can identify subject, occasion, audience, purpose, and speaker, but many of them do so in a shallow manner, not providing enough detail. You could decide to create rubrics of different colors: *Yellow* rubrics assess for the basics; once students master that rubric, they elevate to the *pink* rubrics, which assess beyond the obvious and into the realm of implications of the cartoons. The *white* rubrics elevate to assess beyond the particular cartoon, perhaps requiring students to find other cartoons on the same subject, expressing a different opinion, or to have them find other cartoons by the same commentator, or an editorial on the same subject.

In differentiated instruction practice, preassessment is an ongoing practice, determining how you will recommend remediation and advancement.

Using Technology to Make Tiered Tasking More Effective

As you can see from these examples, technology has numerous applications in making tiered tasks more interesting, imaginative and accessible. In considering what role technology can play when you are designing, organizing, presiding over, and keeping track of students' progress, the following may be helpful:

♦ Balance the tech and the task: If you give the students doing the least sophisticated task the most technology to use, these students may benefit in various ways. Technology is assistive, motivating, and efficient. Allowing students who need work on the fundamentals to use technology to do the *side work*, such as the word processing or presentation, the job can get done faster without detracting from your learning objective.

♦ Use your Web site to assign tasks: Especially if you are assigning tasks based on preassessment information (rather than having students choose), you might want to protect students' privacy by assigning tasks through e-mail.

♦ Establish Command Central: Students are likely to be working out of the library or computer room. Even if they are all in the classroom, you might want them to check in with their questions to you, and yours to them, through your Web site. This works well if you have learning stations, each having a computer for several students to use, as they work in groups.

Support, Opportunity, and Clarity:

We use technology to provide *support* for tiered tasks when students gather information that is presented in different ways on the Internet. Students who are below-grade level readers can be directed to reading material on the topic presented with a comfortable vocabulary level, larger print, numerous illustrations. The Internet, with its multiplicity of Web sites on a topic, offers an array of levels of sophistication about any topic.

Let's say you teach life science. Your students are learning about cell division. If you do a search with the words "cell division" and "learning about," you'll locate excellent sites geared from elementary school through graduate level. Students can place work from the site that has the most accessible language. You can even build beginner, intermediate, and advanced sites into your task structure. The Internet, being highly visual, supports learning through copious illustrations and photography. Tiered tasks with Internet support provide *opportunity* for students for both advancement and review.

As teachers, we use textual features, such as bulleted lists, to present the tasks *clearly*. We provide supplemental information on our own Web sites for students who were absent, or who may need directions to be rephrased. . As we observe how students are working through the task, we adjust our directions, clarifying certain passages, guiding students toward the completion of their tasks. Our Web site, then, becomes an extension of our presence in class. This may sound formidable at first, but, as you become accustomed to working with your own Web site, you'll find that just a few minutes, (and these can be spent during class time as the students are working) can go a very long way in clarifying your expectations.

Common Teacher Concerns About Tiered Tasking

Because tiered tasks are so much a part of differentiated instruction, I do spend a great deal of time in my workshops explaining them and offering time for teachers to construct them. I like to be able to take their drafts home with me, comment on their clarity and efficacy, and then give them more time to revise. I find that the mindset of tiered task design takes a while to develop; teachers need assistance, feedback, and time to reflect.

I've collected the most common questions and concerns that teachers have about tiered tasking:

♦ Is this something that I'm expected to do all of the time? Should every performance task be tiered?

Because I think of differentiated instruction as something that we do to solve problems, I'd say that we should offer tiered tasks when we have reason to think that there's considerable range in a class's ability to process a certain concept. If everyone can function within a reasonable range for a particular task, why give three tiers? Tiered tasks solve the problem that occurs when students on the high end would be unchallenged if asked to do the same as all of the other students, and when students on the low end need reinforcement.

Usually, a task that would take a week or more to do would be sufficiently complex to warrant tri- or bi-leveling. So, no, I wouldn't expect every, or even most performance tasks to need to be tiered.

Tiered tasks are only one of many ways to differentiate. But some people immediately think of tiered tasks as synonymous with differentiated instruction, and because they don't like tiered tasking, they think differentiated instruction is not for them. The fact is, you can have a class that meets the needs of a variety of learners and offers students appropriate choices without ever having to use the tiered tasks structure.

♦ Tiered tasking seems like an overwhelming amount of work. Why not just give extra credit or remedial assignments?

Tiered tasks, as described here, are a refined version of what we think of as remedial assignments and extra credit. The refinement lies in *quality* over *quantity*: Whereas you might ask for more of the same as extra credit or remediation, a tiered task would require more abstract thinking for advanced students; bringing the concept down to a more concrete level for students needing remediation.

♦ If we give low-level tasks to some students, will they ever be able to move up to where they need to be for the State assessments?

This is important. Tiered tasks shouldn't be thought of as a way to replace remediation. The student who remains at the same level is like someone pedaling on an exercise bike that isn't even engaged to provide any resistance. For students in inclusion classes who are functioning on a literary level, we need to map out how the lower tiers are going to become more demanding (abstract and complex) over time.

♦ How do you know that you are offering high-level tasks?

High level tasks have a high degree of abstraction. They may ask for evaluation against criteria. They require the student to transcend the obvious. Or, they may require multiple steps, synthesis, interdisciplinary thinking. They may be long term, taking extended time to complete. They may require a multiplicity of personal skills such as patience, perseverance, communication, and attention to detail.

♦ I want everyone to do the high level tasks, but some will need more support. Can you have a tiered tasks in which there are different degrees of scaffolding?

You can assign everyone the same high-level task, and provide additional scaffolding for kids who need more support; yes, this is a form of tiering and it works very well!

The Tic Tac Toe Chart

Some teachers like to use a nine-cell chart to present tiered tasks. Using such a chart, you can ask students to choose any combination, and you can attach point values to each cell.

Use the guidelines in Figure 3.1 to construct directions for tasks on three levels. This one is based on Bloom's taxonomy.

Figure 3.1. Tic Tac Toe Chart

Identifying main idea of a single source	Showing a basic understanding of a concept	Recalling information
Organizational task	Analyzing a case study or exemplar	Summarizing from various sources
Synthesizing from different subject areas	Comparison-contrast	Evaluating against criteria

Conclusion

Many educators conjure up an image of tiered tasking when they think of DI. Some even can't think of DI as anything else. I think tiered tasks have advantages and disadvantages, and are one of several, not necessarily the best, paradigms for differentiating instruction. Tiered tasking is hard on the teacher, and probably works best in collaborative classes where there's some division of planning between two teachers. Whether you work in partnership or by yourself, I'd recommend giving your tiered task to a colleague for review before giving it to the students.

4

Unit Menus

This chapter explains what unit menus are and their important role as components of DI. Unit menus should include choices that require technology.

What are Unit Menus? Why Offer Them?

Unit menus are an array of project choices that demonstrate core knowledge. The kinds of projects that we see on unit menus are also known as performance task assessments, alternative assessments, authentic assessments, or project-based learning.

Unit menus might include choices such as these:

- ◆ Skits and scenarios (rehearsed or improvised)
- ◆ Videos, animations, and multimedia productions
- ◆ Exhibits, museum mock-ups
- ◆ Art-related projects
- ◆ Traditional written reports
- ◆ Creative writing
- ◆ WebQuests, Scavenger hunts, and other web-based research projects
- ◆ Maps, charts, diagrams
- ◆ Story boards
- ◆ Interdisciplinary projects
- ◆ Community-based projects involving interviews, surveys, or research into local history
- ◆ Threaded discussions online
- ◆ Panel discussions, debates

- PowerPoint presentations in varying degrees of sophistication
- Creation of board games, including e-games and games created by computer applications, such as Word, Excel, and PowerPoint
- Statistical reports and analyses
- 'Zines
- Simulations and reenactments
- Tour guides, travelogues, brochures, field guides

We offer unit menus so that students can build on their knowledge based on their own strengths, learning styles, and interests. Side benefits are that the class produces a variety of products, many of which can be displayed, presented, or in other ways shared with the class for additional learning reinforcement. Another advantage of unit menus is that the process itself extends the learning of core knowledge into applications and interdisciplinary, creative thinking. A well-designed unit menu offers increased opportunities for active learning and use of cumulative subject area knowledge.

Dos and Don'ts of Unit Menu Design

The key to unit menu design is to remember what we want the unit menu tasks to accomplish (Figure 4.1). Each task choice must

- Be substantial enough to demonstrate knowledge and advance learning for substantial concepts and supportive facts in the subject area
- Require comparable amounts of time and energy as the other tasks
- Be challenging

Figure 4.1. Dos and Don'ts of Unit Menu Design

DO	*DON'T*
Plan around essential questions and thematic unit questions.	Be dazzled by complications in artwork or technology.
Design projects requiring language and improved reading and writing.	Allow students to "work around" reading and writing.
Encourage interdisciplinary connections.	Allow students to choose the same kinds of projects every time.
Encourage personal connections.	Assign simple projects that can be clipped from the Internet.
Encourage connections to social issues.	Assign overly complex projects that will require parental intervention.
Use projects as a means to learn material for traditional testing.	Allow for presentations that eat up too much class time. It may be appropriate to give students a time limit to present key parts of their project.
Lean toward projects that can be presented or displayed.	
Develop a simple rubric.	Overlook the value of humor as a learning outlet, but don't allow the hilarity of a student-made video to digress from the essential questions and fact-based support.
	Eliminate traditional testing.

Limit the Choices

Your unit menu is complete with four or five choices, six at most. An overwhelming array of choices is not only unnecessary work for you, it's actually distracting to the students. Your more ambitious students will waste time fussing about which of a large number of choices they should take; while your struggling students may just give up entirely, feeling overloaded. A paradox of human psychology is that we feel safer and more in control when given a limited number of choices. A large number of choices only makes us feel doubtful that we chose wisely. A dizzying array of choices can be paralyzing, as the Existentialists have pointed out.

Essential Questions
and Thematic Unit Questions

It's important to understand how to base presentation, learning processes, and assessment products on essential questions and thematic unit questions. If you *don't* take the time to think in these terms, then you run the risk of having your unit menu choices be cute, rather than meaningful. The time that your students spend on their projects may not galvanize knowledge that will help them on traditional tests. If done right, I believe that project-based learning can and will elevate test scores, and that the two—project-based, concept-driven learning activities and test-oriented learning—can complement each other. But this will happen only if your unit menu choices are grounded in essential questions and thematic unit questions.

Essential questions are transcendent. They are larger than the exemplar, or "unit," being studied. Thematic questions are also *big ideas*, but they focus more on the exemplar. Here are some examples:

Example 1
Ninth-Grade English Class Reading *Julius Caesar*

Essential Questions	*Thematic Unit Questions*
How do villains operate?	Why does Cassius want to assassinate Caesar? How does he manipulate others, particularly Brutus? What are Cassius's personal traits that contribute to his villainy?
How do honorable people make decisions?	How and why does Brutus decide to join the conspiracy? Who and what influences him?
What are the different kinds of power?	What are the different kinds of power that are portrayed in this play?
How does language change?	What features of Shakespearean language differ from contemporary language?
What is dramatic structure?	What is the dramatic structure of this play?
How does poetic language enhance meaning and intensify drama?	How does poetic language enhance meaning and intensify dramatic effect in particular lines, speeches, and dialogue?

You shouldn't spend much time trying to answer the essential questions themselves: They are too sweeping. The reason for the thematic unit questions is to reign in the scope of the essential questions, to have something to actually work with as we move toward understandings of the essential questions. The essential questions remind us why learning the exemplar, whether that be a work of literature, a period of history, a principle of mathematics, or a hypothesis of science, is worthwhile. Without the essential questions, we just have facts. With the essential questions, we not only have a reason for knowing the facts, we also have a place in our brains to file other facts from other exemplars.

If you use a full-service literature anthology published by one of the major houses, such as *The Elements of Literature* (4th course, published by Holt, Rinehart, and Winston, 2000), you can orient your students to the essential questions by reading the unit introductions. These give students the *why and wherefore* of particular genres and themes. Once you clarify your essential questions and thematic questions for yourself and for your students, you can create unit menus, like this one:

Unit Menu

Choose one of the following projects. Each project should refer specifically to at least five different events in the play. Use quotations to support your assertions. Refer to events from various points in the play.

- *Brutus with Himself at War.* To show that you understand Brutus's mixed emotions and conflicting interests, enact a series of skits (with a partner or solo) in which you portray Brutus expressing his ambivalence prior to the assassination. Set your enactment in a modern setting. Use modern language, with some Shakespearean phrases sprinkled in for effect.

- *Double Image.* To show that you understand how Cassius's words belie his true intent, draw a picture of Cassius (a stick figure is fine). On one side, write his words. On the other side, write his intentions.

- *Mapping.* To show that you understand the play's five-act structure, draw an "action map," showing the climactic moments and the events leading up to them. You may use arrows, hills and valleys, and line intensity or other visual codes to indicate the rise and fall of the action in each act and in the play as a whole. Label your map with specific key lines from the play that represent turning points.

- *Debate.* To show that you understand that the character of Brutus can be looked on in two different perspectives, with a partner, present a formal Lincoln–Douglass debate in which you argue the following resolution: "Brutus is an honorable man."

♦ *Language Analysis.* To show that you understand the special features of Shakespeare's language, select two lines, one speech, and two "quick-fire" dialogue segments from various points in the play. In the first column, write the quotation. In the second column, identify the poetic qualities and what they are called. In the third column, write the effect that this poetic quality has on the audience.

Example 2
Ninth-Grade Social Studies Class Studying the Leadership of Julius Caesar

Essential Questions	*Thematic Unit Questions*
What are the qualities of leadership?	What qualities did Julius Caesar have that made him a strong leader?
What is the difference between a republic and a monarchy?	Why didn't Julius Caesar take the crown? What may have happened if he had?
What are the results of a catastrophic political event, such as assassination?	What were the results of the assassination of Julius Caesar?
Do the times make the leader, or does the leader make the times?	What did Julius Caesar do to change the Roman Empire? What conditions existed that led to his triumphs?
What is the influence of antiquity on Western civilization?	What evidence do we have that modern societies were influenced by antiquity?

Unit Menu

Choose one of the following projects. Each project should refer specifically to your textbook readings, your class notes, and at least one other outside source. Include a bibliography.

♦ *Meet the Press.* To show that you understand the controversies surrounding Julius Caesar's refusal of the crown, enact an interview with Julius Caesar as if he is a guest on Meet the Press. Be sure to ask serious, probing questions that show an understanding of the controversies and important issues of the day. In your questions and answers, refer to other leaders of antiquity that we have learned about.

♦ *Toast.* To show your understanding of the significance of Julius Caesar's conquest over Pompey, write a toast to be delivered in honor of Caesar's triumphant return to Rome. Give specific historical details.

♦ *PowerPoint.* To show that you understand the influence of ancient Rome on several aspects of modern society, make a presentation that includes pictures, video clips, and primary source documents. In your presentation, juxtapose images of modern society next to those representing ancient Rome.

♦ *Debate.* To show that you understand how leadership affects societies, enact a formal Lincoln–Douglass debate in which you argue the following resolution: The assassination of Julius Caesar was politically justified to preserve the republic of Rome.

♦ *Comparison/Contrast.* To show that you understand two historical events and their causes and results, compare and contrast the assassination of Julius Caesar to the assassination of Abraham Lincoln. Express your findings as a Venn diagram or an essay.

Example 3
Level 2 Spanish Class Learning About Direct Objects

Essential Questions	*Thematic Unit Questions*
How do languages use cases?	How does Spanish express pronouns in the objective case?
How does word order in syntax determine meaning?	Where do we place direct objects?
What are the differences and similarities between English and Spanish?	How do I use my knowledge of English syntax to help me express direct objects in the objective case in Spanish?

Unit Menu

To express your understanding of direct objects in Spanish, you may do any of the following. Note that all three choices have two components: speech and writing. Your scenario must be videotaped and viewed by you and your partner, as well as by another classmate.

Here are some communication scenarios:

♦ To show your understanding of how direct object nouns and pronouns are used in Spanish, have a rehearsed conversation in which two people work out a misunderstanding about a price.

♦ To show your understanding of how direct object nouns and pronouns are used in Spanish, have a scripted conversation in which two people discuss possible solutions to a problem.

♦ To show your understanding of how direct object nouns and pronouns are used in Spanish, have an impromptu conversation in which two people disagree about whether a certain item is worth purchasing. (The written version will have to be approximate.)

♦ To show your understanding of how direct object nouns and pronouns are used in Spanish, translate a comic strip that is written in English into Spanish. Act it out.

Requirements: In all of the communication scenarios above, you need to use at least 10 direct objects expressed as various pronouns.

Example 4
Earth Science Class Learning Meteorology (Convection Currents)

Essential Questions	*Thematic Unit Questions*
What are the causes and effects of heat?	How do convection currents cause winds?
What are the causes and effects of currents?	What are the patterns of the phenomenon known as the sea breeze? Why does the sea breeze occur?

Unit Menu

To show your understanding of how convection currents create and affect sea breezes, do one of the following:

♦ *Weather report.* To show your understanding of how convection currents affect sea breezes, give a detailed weather report, along with map, regarding how convection currents will create and affect sea breezes in a particular coastal region, day and night.

♦ *Written report.* To show your understanding of how convection currents affect sea breezes, write a one-page report explaining how convection currents affect sea breezes. Include several specific examples, referring to different regions, day and night.

♦ *Detailed maps.* To show your understanding of how convection currents affect sea breezes, draw several maps that show how convection currents affect sea breezes during the day and at night in two different regions. Carefully label and annotate your maps.

Example 5
A Sixth-Grade Math Class is Learning When to Use Particular Operations

Essential Questions	*Thematic Unit Questions*
What are the ways of putting quantities together and pulling them apart?	What are addition, subtraction, multiplication, and division?
How do we perform these operations?	How do we add, subtract, multiply, and divide?
How do we match an operation to a problem?	When should we add, subtract, multiply, and divide?

Unit Menu

Given 0.7 H 0.34 = 0.238, create a real-life problem that this operation would solve.

Choose one of the following to express your understanding of this problem:

♦ *Skit.* To show your understanding of what a particular operation can do to solve a problem, act out a conversation between two business partners in which the partners work out a problem that, at some point in the problem-solving process, requires all four operations. On your conversation, have one partner clearly explaining the problem, and the other clearly explaining the solution. Include many questions from both partners.

♦ *Word problem.* To show your understanding of what a particular operation can do to solve a problem, write a word problem that requires all four operations at some point in the problem-solving process.

♦ *Manipulatives.* To show your understanding of what a particular operation can do to solve a problem, use beads and show with your hands how each operation can be used to solve a particular kind of problem.

♦ *Pictures.* To show your understanding of what a particular operation can do to solve a problem, draw a diagram illustrating the problem-solving process for each of the four operations.

Conclusion

I think unit menus are easier to design than tiered tasks, because with unit menus you don't have to worry so much about differing levels of depth, complexity, and abstraction. You do, however, have to concern yourself with essential questions and make sure that all choices in the unit menu offer targeted learning experiences. All choices should call for critical thinking, communication, and literacy in your subject area. All choices should show an understanding of a key concept, supported by relevant information.

5

Using Technology to Construct Learning Centers and Stations

This chapter explains the workings of learning centers and stations. Elementary teachers are usually well acquainted with in-class learning centers and learning stations. Secondary teachers may not be familiar with these structures, so here's a primer.

First of all, what are they? Learning centers and stations are places in the classroom where students can find different kinds of materials to support learning in a particular field or to practice a skill. The difference, although both may look the same, lies in how centers and stations are used. A center is a place where the students would find various resources to extend or reinforce their knowledge or skills in a given field. A station is one stop in a series of other stations. A student would be expected to complete work or pass a gateway at a station, and then move on to another station that advances that concept or skill. A learning center is a mini-library where one is expected to linger and explore; a station is more of a means to an end.

Math learning centers are popular. Sixth-grade special education teacher Lisa Hill's math learning center has components that offer practice on the skills of percents, equivalent measures, coordinate graphing, geometric shapes, measurements of angles, statistics, money management, measurement terminology, numeration terminology, and decimals. Students can work individually or in pairs, cooperatively or competitively. The center consists of labeled folders in color-coded levels of difficulty. Students move up the colors; they can work in different colors on different topics, depending on their skill in each topic. When Lisa grades a math test, she puts a colored sticker on the student's papers to indicate the center in which they are to work.

Students choose (or are given) a task card. The task card will have a color and a number: The color indicates the topic (such as geometric shapes, measurement of angles, etc.). The number indicates the level of difficulty. The student, we'll call her Stephanie, picks up one of the purple folders, purple being the designated color for geometric shapes. Stephanie is working on level three (top level) today, based on a recent quiz grade in geometric shape identification. Stephanie has shown readiness to advance from the literal level (she can identify, describe, and name properties of geometric shapes) to the application level. Her task card first directs her to the materials that she will need. Then, Stephanie is to solve a puzzle by constructing an origami fish, the directions for which are written in the language of geometry.

Stephanie can take as much time as she needs to complete her task, but she needs to report her progress at the end of the period to the teacher aide. Off-task behaviors are noted. When her task is completed, she will place a purple sticker on the master chart, and write the number "3" on it.

You can surmise that learning centers and stations take time, care, and expense to construct. Most teachers start small, building from year to year just as you'd build your repertoire of stories, examples, and assignments from year to year. Some excellent resources for building learning centers are available from Evan-Moor Educational Publishers. These are books designed for elementary teachers, but secondary teachers can get ideas from them. They provide directions and materials for folders which students would take back to their seats, facilitating the classroom management of running a learning center.

When would stations be preferable to centers? When you have information that students will process at differing paces, you might want to set up stations, each having a gateway, a task or test, to signal readiness to move to the next level. In Stephanie's social studies class, the topic is Colonial America. Stephanie's teacher, Alex Suarez, has done a whole-class introduction to the topic and then has launched the class on a multi-step adventure into the period. At each station, Stephanie will read textual information and apply her knowledge to a timeline, a map, a personal narrative, a terminology page, and a graphic organizer that summarizes the information at the station. Successful completion of the graphic organizer is the passport to the next station. The stations are set up so that Stephanie is going to need her completed packet from the last station to function in the present one. She will have to use her own work as a resource as she goes along.

Be careful of creating pseudo-differentiation through stations. Some teachers set up stations which students visit, do a given piece of a project, and then move on after a set interval. This is a "stations" model, but not a differentiated one. Differentiation can occur through the use of learning stations when any (not necessarily all) of the following conditions is present:

◆ The interval of time that Jessica spends at a given station is not fixed. She can have the time that she needs.

♦ The interval of time is fixed, but the amount of the task that Jessica completes is not necessarily the same as what Justin has completed.

♦ The interval of time and the amount of the task are fixed. However, Jessica can choose from a variety of modes of learning at the station. For example, she has to answer questions about cell division, but she can use a textbook, or a computer, or a review book, or an audio tape to receive the information.

♦ The interval of time, the amount of the task, and the mode of learning are fixed. However, Jessica can choose her own method of showing what she knows. For example, she can answer questions on paper, write a narrative, draw a labeled diagram, or make up a study guide.

Using PowerPoint to Create Learning Centers and Stations

Physical learning centers and stations are more commonly found in elementary classrooms than in secondary classrooms. Many high school teachers don't have autonomy over classroom space. For some reason, many of the commercially available materials to establish learning centers have an elementary school feel. And most secondary teachers don't have the training for utilizing classroom space in innovative ways. Thus, PowerPoint and Web-based centers are ideal for secondary teachers.

Why Use Centers?

Why set up learning centers, rather than just doing whole-class instruction? Whole-class instruction is the efficient model for the lecture/presentation format. We usually have whole-class instruction when we introduce new factual information, explain new procedures, explain solutions to problems that every member of the class has done, and orchestrate class discussions. Whole-class instruction has its shortcomings in that many students don't actively participate. Students working at a center are likely to be actively engaged with the language and thinking of the subject. Centers are the efficient model for the following:

♦ *Reinforcing and reviewing.* Casy's biology class has a unit test tomorrow on cell division. Casy was absent for two of the lecture days. Although he read the chapter in the text and copied his lab partner's notes, Casy appreciates using part of class time to work at the study center. In this study center, Casy's teacher has made past test questions and answers available.

- *Bringing the learning to a less complex, more concrete level.* Becca has trouble understanding theories in her economics class. She can get it if the explanations are example-based, rather than theoretical. Becca's teacher has set up a center equipped with manipulatives that represent the economic elements of a society. As Becca and Sarah work with these manipulatives, they help each other understand supply side economics in a way that words and graphics alone couldn't accomplish.

- *Applying the learning to investigations, cases, and problems.* Kevin, Brianna, and Kumar track their mock investments in the Stock Exchange center of their economics class.

- *Advancing the learning to more sophisticated levels of depth and complexity.* Justin is a math whiz. He works in the engineering center of his math class, applying concepts to architecture.

- *Adjusting the learning mode for students with special needs.* Nathan uses headphones to listen to his favorite music while he takes his math test. Nathan needs his music to get into a zone where he won't be distracted.

- *Socializing the learning.* Stacia learns by talking. She and Alison do their math homework together in the math learning center.

Why E-Centers?

Physical centers and stations take up space, consume materials, require set-up and take-down, and cleanup. E-centers require only a computer. Additionally, a student working on a computer has privacy: No one needs to know that he is doing remedial or basic work.

Unlike physical centers, e-centers are portable (for students who have to miss school) and easily adjustable on a disk or CD. You can monitor e-center work on screen, eliminating folders and piles of papers. E-centers accomplish the same objectives as physical centers, but without the need for clotheslines and clothespins, plastic bags, shoeboxes, and color-coded folders.

Whenever we turn to a technological solution, we need to ask ourselves three questions:

1. Does the technological version of my lesson offer a true advantage over the traditional version? The obvious advantage of an e-center over a physical center is its practicality, as detailed above. But, furthermore, e-centers allow you to accommodate learners with special needs much more readily than physical centers do. With an e-center designed on PowerPoint, you can adjust the font and im-

ages to accommodate students with special visual needs. You can use the various organizational aides such as charts, tables, and inserted graphics to help students who depend on visual aides. Some students are overwhelmed by the size of a task. Screen-based presentations allow them to focus on one screen at a time.

2. Does the technology simplify what needs to be simplified, and elevate what needs to be elevated? Caroline, a seventh-grade student, is using a PowerPoint learning center to review key events in the Civil War and understand their significance. The PowerPoint presentation guides her as she writes a series of headlines that tell the story of the Civil War. Each screen has skeletal textual information (Caroline has already been exposed to the details through her textbook and through lecture and class notes), along with a photograph and a URL for further information, should she need it. Caroline is a student with reading deficits. This learning center is appropriate for her learning needs because the volume of text is not overwhelming, yet she does have to read and write, showing that she has extracted basic information and can put it in the specialized language of headlines. The way this learning center is set up, Caroline will intersperse the existing screens (that were, in fact, created by another student) with her headlines. The essential question that guides this learning experience is: "What were the key events in the Civil War? How did these key events change the course of the war?" For Caroline, this format simplified the information while elevating her thinking skills, as she considered that the function of headlines is to make readers interested, using as few words as possible.

    This same learning center is used differently for other students. Once the students take control of the PowerPoint presentation (by copying it onto their own files), they can add, rearrange, or change the slides. Another student can take Caroline's headlines and write news reports. Another can write journal entries. Another can insert more photographs, pulled from the Internet. As students visit the learning center, the PowerPoint presentation can grow. The teacher then saves different forms of it. She can show these new forms to the whole class, have students explain their additions, and even use the new versions in future years.

3. Am I using the technology to its proper advantage, or am I just creating an onscreen workbook? As we see from the example above, an e-center created on PowerPoint can be far more than an onscreen workbook. Workbooks can't invite students to change and recombine them. Inasmuch as workbooks are static and PowerPoint pre-

sentations are flexible, e-centers have the potential to offer far more active learning.

Transitioning to E-Centers

If you already have physical centers established, transitioning to e-centers is going to take some time and work. But the time invested will save you time in the end, as you won't have to tend to the maintenance of a physical center that runs out of materials and has to be constantly reorganized.

Although we usually think of PowerPoint is a visual aide used for oral presentations, here we use PowerPoint as a learning center. If you are creating a PowerPoint learning center, start small, perhaps with only ten slides. Leave room for students to add slides as they work on the center. Their slides can be interspersed or added to the end. Interspersed slides will provide supplementary detail. Add-ons will extend the information. Think of your PowerPoint learning center as a work in progress. Begin with text only, or just a few pictures. Elaborate in the future, using your students' contributions, to add URLs, additional graphics, audio and video clips, and more information.

Here are some tips for creating an effective PowerPoint presentation:

♦ *Keep it simple, visually and textually.* Remember that PowerPoint is an effective summarizer. If you want complex sentences, PowerPoint is probably not the way to go.

♦ *Remember that color is a learning tool.* We tend to associate ideas together that are presented in the same color. Keep this in mind as you choose your color backgrounds. And remember that a background is just that. Don't allow colors to eclipse information.

♦ *Avoid clutter.* Avoid unnecessary special effects. Remember that students with learning deficits often have difficulty sorting the important facts from the details.

♦ *Strive for visual unity.* Don't use too many different fonts or styles.

♦ *Background and foreground main information and subordinate information accordingly.*

♦ *Consider carefully the appropriateness of your visuals, in terms of the tone that they convey.* Cartoons, animations, sound, video, and clip art are fun and motivating. They can bring to life an otherwise dry topic. However, be mindful that a serious topic should not be trivialized by frivolous effects.

Before you go to the trouble of transforming an existing learning center, you might want to take the time to evaluate it. Learning centers, whether physical or electronic, are only as valuable as the quality learning that they provide. Consider these questions about the value of your learning center experiences:

- Does it provide opportunities for higher level thinking, such as creativity, analysis, synthesis, and evaluation?

- Does it improve the student's language skills, whether the student reads on a college level or has serious deficits?

- Does it allow for divergent thinking?

- Does it strengthen skills and advance understanding?

Audio Centers

It was William Congreve, and not, as 'tis often thought, William Shakespeare, who penned the words "Music hath charms to soothe the savage breast/ to soften rocks/ to bend the knotted oak." Music, rhythm, and the spoken word can be a powerful learning aide or reward.

Audio learning centers provide headphones so that students can either learn information by listening to it, or listen to music while learning. Some people perform better on fine motor tasks while listening to music. A 1994 study that was done at the State University of New York at Buffalo (JAMA 1994; 272(22): 1724) found that many surgeons heightened their concentration and lowered their stress levels by listening to the music of their choice while performing surgery.

Other people find that their concentration improves, or even requires, absolute silence. The modern classroom is abuzz with student talk and a multitude of stimuli. Some students may benefit from blocking out ambient sounds through the use of headphones that play "white noise."

Here is a summary of the basic tenets of music therapy. Although music therapists typically work in therapeutic environments, much of what they know about the emotional and intellectual impact of music and rhythm is useful for teachers:

- Singing: People who have difficulty with speech fluency are often helped by singing. Choral singing builds community. When we learn information to a tune, we tend to remember it for a long time. And singing can help people learn and remember sequences.

- Rhythmic movement creates muscle memory, which is a very durable form of memory.

- Listening to one's choice of music offers a sense of autonomy to oppositional students, and to students who simply need to retreat into their own worlds occasionally. Because of its ability to evoke memories and associations, music can help the learner make long-lasting links to the information that accompanied the music. Music can put the listener into an imaginative frame of mind. And listeners to music of a given culture achieve a special humanistic understanding of that culture.

Music, listened to or created, has a powerful effect on the mind. Music connects to emotion; emotion connects to learning. Music also connects to mathematics, personal identity, muscle memory, culture, and community.

Another use for listening centers is tape-assisted reading. In tape-assisted reading, the reader reads along with the tape. Tape-assisted reading is important for deficit readers to improve their skills. Deficit readers, because they lack fluency, lose the meaning of text by the time they finish decoding and processing. With tape-assisted reading, the deficit reader hears the proper pacing, phrasing, pronunciation, and emphasis, all the while improving sight vocabulary. It is important to remember that the tape-assisted reader is receiving all of the information, just as an independent reader would do. Students who would benefit from tape-assisted reading are those who are dyslexic, those with attention deficits, and the visually impaired.

Web-Based Centers

A Web-based learning center or station can be a classroom Web site, a WebQuest, a hotlist, a source of prescriptive lessons, or research project. Some teachers like to use a more appealing name for the latter: treasure hunts, scavenger hunts, digs, missions, expeditions, or shopping sprees.

Classroom Web sites should be more than onscreen bulletin boards. A good classroom Web site can function as an extension of the life of the class itself:

- A showcase of student work. (Never use a student's full name on the Internet. Identify students by first name or initials only.)

- A classroom library, consisting of links to reference materials and related readings.

- A place to find prescriptive (differentiated) lessons in response to demonstrated student need.

- A communications center between teacher and student and teacher and parents.

- A communications center among teachers, and between your students and teachers of the same subject other than you.

WebQuests: WebQuests are inquiry-based learning experiences in which students solve problems and research information by using specific Internet sites that the teacher has directed them to.

Hotlists: Like WebQuests, hotlists are lists of Internet sites that the teacher has put together for a specific purpose. A hotlist differs from a WebQuest in that a hotlist is part of a WebQuest. (In working through a WebQuest, the student will use a hotlist to find information.)

Prescriptive Lessons: These are lessons, puzzles, or other learning experiences that students can do on their own to address demonstrated needs. They can be skill-based or information-based.

How to Build a Learning Center

To adapt the Grammar Hardware Store learning center to a topic in your own subject area, you'd first need to consider the features of this learning center:

- ◆ *Taxonomy in a subject.* The Grammar Hardware Store is about a taxonomy. All subjects have taxonomies: classifications, properties, and terminology. Understanding the taxonomy is basic to higher level thinking in that subject. To understand a taxonomy, we need to know terminology, classifications, and hierarchical relationships. The following are some subject area taxonomies to which you could adapt the Grammar Hardware Store learning center:

  - *Branches of American government*

    Essential Questions. What are the functions of the three branches of government? What is their relationship to one another? How do the three branches achieve checks and balances?

    Advancements. How are each of the three branches organized within themselves? Track a particular contemporary issue, showing how it relates to the three branches of government.

  - *World religions.* What are the foundational beliefs and practices of the major religions of the world? What is the relationship between religion and geography?

  - Advancements

  - Geographical regions

  - Life forms (kingdom, phylum, class, order, species)

  - Rocks and minerals: properties, regions, industrial uses

  - Molecular and atomic structure

  - Mythology

  - Genres of literature

- Properties of numbers

- Geometric entities

- AR, ER, IR verbs in Spanish

- Dialects: regions, pronunciations, social class

- Principles of physical science

- Parts of a car

- Departments of a business organization

When it comes to taxonomies, at the secondary level, you have found that students come to you with varying degrees of understanding. Some have memorized terms without a deep understanding; some have gaps; some have learned what you consider outdated taxonomies; and some are ready for refinements and ambiguities.

♦ *Finding a metaphor.* The metaphor of a hardware store works well for grammar because we use grammatical concepts to build language, and because we think of a hardware as being so well-arranged, carrying many variations on a basic tool or embellishment. Metaphors are important for taxonomic learning because the learner can latch onto a familiar pattern. Any familiar structure that relies on an organizational pattern—stores and malls, kitchens, chests of drawers, offices and buildings—make good metaphors for taxonomies.

♦ *You have your taxonomy and your metaphor.* Now you are ready to structure your learning center. I suggest cartoons, and I've used ClipArt.com, which holds a vast array of clever, eye-catching cartoon graphics on every subject imaginable. The visuals are important in maintaining interest and relating to the metaphor. I divided the grammatical information into three major categories, the first of which is basic, the second two of which are interchangeable. Present your information skeletally, which is the format in which PowerPoint works best. You may want to print out space for side notes, so that students can add supplemental information and examples.

♦ *Decide on the activities that students will do as they go through the learning center.* Will they answer questions as they go along? Give examples? Draw diagrams to show their understanding? Rephrase? Do practice exercises? How will students interact with the information so that they own it? An effective learning center has opportunities for various learning styles: visuals, auditory, socialization, and manipulatives.

♦ *Differentiation by ability.* In the Grammar Hardware Store, my base-line is Aisle One. Only students who have mastered Aisle One can proceed, but not everyone has to proceed beyond Aisle One. Some students are going to need the entire time allotted to this unit of study to get through Aisle One, and those students will have advanced their learning about grammar tremendously by doing so. For students on an entry level to leave my class knowing the parts of speech and how they fit into a form and serve a function would be a creditable accomplishment, no doubt. So, one way of looking at differentiation is through the relationship between pace and content: Given a certain amount of time, students will reach different levels in the taxonomy. The important thing is that the advancing students have actually advanced their learning, not that they've just done more of the same.

The higher levels of your learning center should address more sophisticated facets of the taxonomy:

- *Refinements and subtleties.* Discerning more and more subcategories that recognize finer differences.

- *Ambiguities and overlaps.* Although the purpose of a taxonomy is to place specimens in categories, sophisticated learners can handle exceptions, marginalities, gray areas: In grammar, for example, a participle is a verb in form and an adjective in function. In Constitutional law, we make judgments as to whether or not the Supreme Court has a right to rule on particular issues, such as Roe v. Wade.

- *Putting the taxonomy to use.* Now that we know what everything is called and where it belongs, how can we use this information to solve problems?

♦ *Management of the learning center.*

Where and what are the benchmarks? What is Plan B if the student goes through the activities in the learning center more than once and still is not ready to move on? The Grammar Hardware Store learning center is sequential: You go through Aisle One, then Two, then Three (actually, two and three are interchangeable). If you had a learning center about the taxonomy of government, for example, it might not operate in the same way. The executive branch is not necessarily more complex than the legislative or the judiciary. In taxonomies where the parts are of similar complexity, you would want the baseline to be that the students have some knowledge of all three branches of government before moving on to more detailed knowledge. So you might organize your slides according to complexity, rather than "finishing" one branch of government before moving on. It might look like this:

Slides 1–6: Present the basics of the three branches of government

Slides 7–18: Present subcategories such as presidential cabinet posts, congressional committees, or lower courts

Slides 19–21: Present case studies of social problems and where they belong in the governmental structure

Conclusion

Learning centers and stations can be converted into Web sites and PowerPoint presentations for secondary classrooms. Using technology to create and maintain learning centers eliminates the need for space and architectural features that secondary classrooms, boxy as they are, generally don't have. Think in terms of subjects that students already have some familiarity with, but need review, while other students are ready to handle detail and subtlety. Offer alternatives to provide for different learning styles, especially socialization and multisensory learning in the centers.

6

Differentiated Instruction in Whole-Class Instruction

When you plan differentiation, a module of instruction should be directed to the whole class. Whole-class instruction is the usual method of introducing new information. Think of the lesson cycle as having three branches: introduction of information, constructivist activity, and assessment. Although we usually conceive of the first part of the lesson cycle as whole-class instruction, and the second and maybe third as lending themselves to differentiation, this chapter will present paradigms in which whole-class instruction and differentiation appear in various modules of the learning cycle.

Introduction of Information

When we introduce information, we need to find ways to connect it to what the student already knows. Learning can only be absorbed in layers. We may want to differentiate the way we invite students to connect new information to existing information. We can do this by encouraging students, in whole-class instruction, to make a personal connection between the new information and their lives.

Susan Kline teaches eighth-grade math. She introduces probability by giving students fortune cookies. But the kind of fortune cookies she uses are ordinary cookies out of a box in which she has inserted messages like "We will have a snow day next week," "The basketball team will go to States," and other messages that her students will be interested in. She then asks them how they would go about figuring out the chances of having their fortune come true. This is whole-class instruction, designed to show students the applicability of the mathematical concepts which will soon be presented in abstractions. As the unit proceeds, students continue to apply formulas to their fortunes, but the formulas become more complex as the instruction and learning progress.

Whole-Class Instruction
in the Collaborative-Inclusion Class

In a *collaborative-inclusion* class, a substantial number of special education students are placed in the regular class academic class. Usually, a special education teacher collaborates with the subject area teacher in planning the lessons. The planning takes into account that all students need to reach high standards, but some may need adjustments to content, process, and assessments. The class may be supplemented with additional time for the special education teacher to provide learning support and modifications. Ideally, the special education teacher and the subject area teacher have designated mutual preparation time.

The collaborative-inclusion model is one of the main reasons why teachers and administrators are interested in learning about DI. In fact, I've found in my staff development work that it is the inclusion class that administrators have in mind when they think of DI. But without the proper vision, planning, and support, this model can fail to meet its mission of providing high level education to students with special learning needs. The idea is *not* to create two classes housed in the same room. Nor is the idea for the inclusion class to become a special education class, with the *regular* kids there, as though brought in by central casting, to *set the example*. For that matter, the inclusion class is not supposed to ignore the fact that a substantial number of students are going to have a particularly hard time comprehending the material, concentrating on the lesson, and expressing what they know. Special education students placed in an inclusion class are likely to have problems with language, socialization, study skills, and attentiveness. They need a class that has lots of reinforcement, multisensory engagement, structured socialization, and establishment of expectations. Students with special needs, whether those be emotional or intellectual, are going to need lots of scaffolding.

Inclusion can work well if the teachers understand how to differentiate instruction without sacrificing the concept. As with all differentiated instruction, you need to focus on the *concept* as you plan how different kinds of learners are going to show an understanding of it. Secondary classes are very much driven by content. Teachers have great concerns about balancing the need to teach a great deal of content with the need to give students time to process. Teachers are interested in knowing how to address various learners while doing whole-class instruction. This chapter will discuss how something called the *modified lecture format* works, and how putting your lecture on PowerPoint can help you use technology to differentiate instruction.

The Modified Lecture Format

When you read my description of the modified lecture format, you are likely to say, "I do that. I didn't know there was a name for it." Or, you may say, "That's something like what I've been trying to do, but now I understand how to refine it into this format." In either case, the point is that you already have knowledge and skill in using this effective technique of delivering whole-class instruction.

In a nutshell, the modified lecture format has three parts: a prelecture piece, wherein students summon prior knowledge and establish expectations for the new information; a 15 minute lecture, with multiple visuals; a 15 minute postlecture time, a debriefing, in which students use their best learning style to "keep" what they've learned. If you do a search on "modified lecture format" you will see how popular it is at the university level. Actually, the traditional university lecture consisted of readings that you were expected to do on your own, followed by a traditional lecture in a lecture hall during which you'd take notes, and then a follow-up break out group led by a teaching assistant. At those sessions, you'd make sense of the lecture by applying its information to cases and by socializing the learning. The modified lecture format condenses that sequence, paying more attention to how to make it more learner friendly.

PowerPoint
for the Modified Lecture Format

Now is the time to start converting your favorite lectures into a PowerPoint presentation. Don't think you have to rework all of your lectures in one year. Make the conversion a three to five year plan. Start small, with a limited number of slides at first. You can build on these lectures from year to year, adding all kinds of graphics and media clips.

In addition to using your PowerPoint lectures in class, here's how you can use them to help students in special circumstances:

♦ You can hand students a disk with the PowerPoint lecture when they've returned from an absence, or when they need to be absent from school for an extended period of time.

♦ You can give the special education teacher a copy of your lecture, so that she can work with students in a resource room.

♦ You can give the disk to accelerated students, and ask them to extend or add detail to the presentation.

♦ You can adjust the level of detail of the presentation to meet the needs of a given class.

♦ You can provide visuals and graphics with your presentation.

When you have a PowerPoint presentation, you can display its contents as a slide show to accompany your live lecture. You can give students notes pages, expecting them to write summaries, key words, questions, or connections in the spaces provided next to each slide.

I have a tendency to wander when I lecture. As a teacher, it's a challenge for me to stay focused and organized. I'm anecdotal and metaphorical in my teaching style. When I take courses, I tend to learn the most from the incidentals, the side trips. If my students are compatible with this teaching style, then they're lucky. If not (and many children and adults are not) then they find me disorganized, and my class frustrates them. Much as I love staying in my own comfort zone (don't we all?), I sometimes have to force myself to adhere to an outline. PowerPoint presentations help me do this. I distribute copies of the notes pages (or outline format) and that helps me keep myself on the straight and narrow. (I wouldn't want to be on the straight and narrow all the time; but some topics are best explained in a linear manner, and I need help with these.)

A classroom library of PowerPoint presentations can be available for study, review, and remediation. These can be housed in the classroom, or in the school's library, even in the public library. They can include a bibliography of online sources of supplemental information.

Modernize Your Handouts

If you know the importance of visuals, if you have the technology to enhance meaning with everything from scanned photography to cartoon images to different font sizes, why do your handouts still look the same way they did when you first began teaching?

Get a copy of *USA Today*. What are its visual features and how do these features not only invite you into the information, but also help you to care about it and remember it?

You're thinking, "Another great idea that I don't have time for." Well, first of all, no one is saying that every single handout has to be a work of art. But if you have a three-year plan to redesign your handouts, a few each semester, you can make a lot of progress. Also, what would happen if your students took your lackluster handouts and did some makeover work? If students can learn by doing something that would improve learning for everyone else, why not have them do it?

Four Whole-Class Projects

Any of the following projects can be created through PowerPoint or Hyperstudio, or online using Filamentality or Web-n-Flow.

♦ Create Virtual Museums

A museum is a collection of items that are of lasting interest because of their role in the story of humankind. Each item is captioned. The museum is organized into exhibits. Create the American Museum of Mathematics or the Metropolitan Museum of Chemistry, with each student responsible for one exhibit. Each exhibit must have a given number of visuals with captions that attract and inform the visitor. There should be rhyme and reason to the order in which the items in the exhibit are presented.

In addition to the exhibits (which can be cooperative ventures), some students should be assigned to peripheral tasks, such as advertising and promoting the museum, creating a brochure, designing the façade of the building, soliciting funding, and so forth.

♦ Create Virtual Zoos

A zoo is a collection of mini-habitats for living things. The zoo is organized into ecosystems. The designer of the zoo must consider the botanical details of each habitat, temperature and light control, and spatial allotments. The premier zoos often have special exhibits, such as the famous Pandas of the San Diego Zoo. Create the Great Zoo of the Earth, consisting of a compilation of some of the great exhibits from all over the world. Each student will be responsible for a particular habitat and a brief explanation of the real zoo from which it comes. As with the Virtual Museum. Some students can do the peripheral and promotional tasks of zoo-making.

♦ Create Virtual Field Trips to the Great Cities of Past and Present

The Virtual Field Trip requires no permission slip. Students create grand field trips, putting together virtual tours of every place from Ancient Rome to the Solar System. Each student is responsible for a particular part of the trip, including lunch and transportation.

♦ Create Virtual Expeditions

The Gold Rush, the Oklahoma Land Rush, or the Lewis and Clarke Expedition can be recreated with a virtual expedition. Each student is responsible for a leg of the journey. Include logs written by various expeditioners with various perspectives and agendas.

To enrich these projects, include the following:

- Music
- Video clips
- Interviews

Real-Time Data Projects

Science, math, and business teachers having students doing real-time data projects such as tracking, including

- Hurricane tracking
- Locating fish by tracking fishing boats in various coordinates
- Marketing trends, tracking inventory

Conclusion

Secondary education is largely based on whole-class instruction. Whole-class instruction is easiest when the class is homogeneous; however, with some imagination and adaptations, it is possible to use technology so as to make whole-class instruction meaningful for students at various levels.

7

Differentiating Traditional Tests

Although differentiated instruction (DI) usually tends toward performance tasks and process learning, traditional tests are an important part of learning in secondary schools, and test-taking differentiation must be addressed. Technology offers students several means for effective study, and it offers teachers ways to differentiate fact-based tests without sacrificing standardized content. The first part of this chapter shows how to help your students study by using technology. The second part shows how to use traditional tests diagnostically, and then how to differentiate test questions by managing a question bank.

Technology for Better Studying

Students can reinforce and scaffold their learning by using the Internet as a study guide. On their own, or working from a list of suggested sites, they can locate the Web site that explains information in the way that works best for them. This may be a site that is rich with visuals, on a lower reading level, offering FAQs on the topic, or that allows online communications.

Some students may form chat room study groups. These study groups should function independently, but you can post questions or pose problems. If your school has a service that hosts a message board, you can use it not only to answer students' questions, but to post guiding questions to direct study.

One disadvantage of technology is that we feel sometimes that we never are off duty. Be sure to make it clear to your students that you are not "on call" except for specified times. Don't entertain e-mail by students or parents (or colleagues or administrators, for that matter) through your personal address. However, you shouldn't overlook the advantages of being able to answer a few quick questions that may save you time in the long run.

Determining Learning Needs
Through Item Analysis

Simple uses of word processing or data base technology can make it possible for you to build up a rich supply of test questions.

If you're lucky, you'll have tests available that already have a useful item analysis. By *item analysis*, we mean: What kinds of questions is the student getting wrong? You could do item analysis in two ways: by *content* and by *question type*.

To do item analysis by content, let's say that an eighth-grade social studies teacher, Dave Hart, gives a unit test on the Great Depression era. Thirty-three questions are broken down as follows:

- 10 multiple choice, asking for factual information (25 points)

- 13 multiple choice, asking for recognition and interpretation of documents studied in class

- 10 constructed response questions, requiring students to answer in complete sentences. The questions require students to explain cause and effect and to synthesize information.

Dave wants the students to continue learning about the items that they missed on the test, but he doesn't want to reteach the information or spend very much more class time on this topic. This is a departmentalized test, as are all unit tests in Dave's school. Teachers are expected to give five unit tests in this format each quarter. These tests were already in place when Dave entered this department.

To item analyze by content, Dave matches the questions to the particular segments of the textbook on which they are based. The unit presents information chronologically:

- Economic trends of the 1920s

- The Wall Street crash

- The Dust Bowl

- Automation

- The Hoover Administration

- The Labor movement of the 1930s

- FDR and the New Deal

Dave scans the test into the word processor and runs a search for key words to locate items in these categories. He then uses the tables format to make a chart on which *the students* will represent their own wrong answers. It looks like this:

The Great Depression Test

Directions: The following chart (Figure 7.1) represents the kinds of questions that were on your test. Circle the questions that you got wrong.

Figure 7.1. Great Depression Test Chart

Topic	Questions							
Economic Trends of the 1920s	25	2	8	15		27		21
The Wall Street Crash of 1929					3	7	20	30
The Dust Bowl	1		26	14			18	5
Automation		24	13			19	33	
The Hoover Administration	23		16		31		6	12
The Labor Movement of the 1930s				4		28	11	29
FDR and the New Deal		32	22	9	10		17	

Can you see a pattern? Now, you have to do some reading in the areas where you got the most wrong.

The three topics in which I need the most relearning are: _____, _____, _____.

Rx: Now that you know exactly where you need the most relearning, you need to follow this procedure:

♦ Locate the pages on which this material is explained in the textbook.

♦ Then, choose one of the following repairs:

• Reread the section and write a Harvard outline.

• Reread the section and write 10 questions. Use the Who? What? When? Where? Why? How? format. Use a variety of question types. Include an answer key that has the pages on which the answers are located.

• Reread the section and draw a detailed diagram or map that explains its key points. You may draw more than one diagram or map.

• Reread the section and make one or more graphic organizers (you may download these from the graphic organizer collection on the class Web site). Use the graphic organizers to express the key information.

- Reread the section and make a poster for the class that expresses the key information. Your poster must be neat, attractive, and easy to read.

- Reread the section and make a study tape of the key information.

- Reread the section and make a PowerPoint presentation expressing the key information. Use authentic pictures.

Dave could decide to item analyze by question type. To do this, he would consider question types such as

♦ Detail questions

♦ Terminology questions

♦ Cause and effect questions

♦ Synthesis questions

Analysis of question type differs from analysis of content in two ways: First, you will find more ambiguity in the questions. They are not so easy to categorize. Second, the questions are qualitatively different. The stronger the student, the better they can handle questions calling for higher-level thinking, such as linking cause and effect and forming synthesized ideas. Dave would want his students to analyze their wrong answers using a chart similar to the one above. The categories would be *detail, terminology, cause and effect,* and *synthesis.* Differentiated follow-up activity would look like this:

Directions to the Students

After you've filled in your chart for analyzing your answers, you need to do the following repairs (Figure 7.2). If you have more than five detail or terminology questions wrong, you need to do column 1 activities. If you have fewer than five detail or terminology questions wrong, then you need to do column 2 activities. Choose one activity from your designated column.

Figure 7.2. Repairs Chart

Repairs for Detail and Terminology

- Make a detailed chart of who, what, where, when, and why information from the chapter.
- Make a timeline based on information in the chapter. Provide names and places for the key events on the timeline.
- Write a Who's Who in the Great Depression chart. For each person, provide information including dates and events
- Make a collection of flashcards to review information about the Great Depression. Each flash card should include a key term on the front, and full detailed information on the back.
- Make a Power Point presentation, giving key terms and events of the Great Depression.

Repairs for Cause & Effect and Synthesis

- Make a cause and effect chart, showing how several events in the Great Depression are linked.
- Write a series of letters from Americans in various social positions, regions, and walks of life, explaining how their lives are being affected by the Depression. Be sure that your letters include specific as well as general information.
- From the Internet, find and print several significant primary historical documents and put them together in a folder. On the back of each document, write a brief explanation of its significance.

Organizing Your Test

Creating Question Banks

Item analysis is meticulous work. Here are some ways to make it less time consuming and durable enough to justify the effort.

- ♦ Teachers of the same course can build a data base of questions for the department. Such a data base can be organized by question type or content so that teachers can pull out questions to differentiate a test, a review sheet, or post-test remediation.

- ♦ You can place questions within a limited number of categories, reducing the amount of time it takes to sort them. Begin with the coarsest divisions, maybe just two or three of them. Next year, you can refine your analysis.

♦ Have *students* do the categorizing of test items after they've taken the test. This activity is an excellent way to review information. Students learn more than just the content by doing this; they also learn the inner workings of test construction. They get inside the language, developing an understanding of the diction and syntax of a test.

♦ There's software available to facilitate test construction (try QuizStar).

Building Tests for Differentiation

Over time and with collaboration, we can build extensive data bases that can be put together to create customized tests for different types of learners. In secondary education, we are concerned about test security. Students use the grapevine to pass along test questions from one period to another, from one year to another. We are constantly concerned about copying when we give a test in class.

Beyond these mundane security concerns, we are also concerned that reading deficits and time constraints compromise the validity of our test results. Although it is true that reading comprehension issues are an intrinsic part of learning in our subjects, we would like to discern what our students actually know about the subject, apart from their ability to process a written test within a limited amount of time.

Consider the kinds of items on a traditional test, and how these can be mixed and matched:

♦ *Multiple choice.* Multiple choice tests are heavily dependent on a student's ability to read complex sentences. A complex sentence is one that has at least two clauses, one of which has to be subordinate. Often, there is multiple subordination in the syntax of a multiple choice test. This is fine for the skillful reader. Think about what the struggling reader has to do. She has to think about new material and wrestle with sentence complexity, and keep four possible sentence finishers in her short term memory all at once. To ease the way for the struggling reader without dumbing down the test, consider the following modifications:

  • Present the question and the choices in as few words as possible. Be mindful of syntactical complexity.

  • Avoid negation as much as possible. The mind processes positive statements more easily than negative ones.

  • Have as much parallel structure in the answer choices as possible.

- Use ordinary vocabulary as much as possible, except for your subject area terms. If elevated vocabulary is necessary, give students a vocabulary list beforehand, consisting of the ordinary (not subject area) words that you expect them to know. Doing so will also cut down on the barrage of "What does _____ mean?" questions that create a nuisance during test time.

- Don't forget that phrases are also vocabulary issues. Phrases such as "in terms of" and "all things being equal" cause the academically sophisticated reader no trouble, but they can be baffling to the struggling reader.

♦ *True/False.* Many people blow off true/false tests as easy, because you have an even chance of guessing right, but I'm one who finds true/false tests difficult. The brain processes statements as true. Therefore, your brain has to do a little flip-flop to realize that a statement is false and then identify it as such. Also, true/false language tends to use a lot of negation. If the item is false and contains negation, your brain has to work overtime on the logic. True/false tests are not kind to the struggling reader or to the student who gets particularly nervous about tests.

♦ *Matching.* Matching columns are favorable to the struggling reader because they use a minimal amount of language.

♦ *Sentence completions.* The caveat about sentence completions is their ambiguity. The stem has to be constructed so that a single response is cued. Another sticking point is that sentence completions require legible handwriting, a problem exacerbated when students are in a rush. Always provide lines and adequate spaces for handwritten responses. Be prepared to spend time deciphering answers.

♦ *Labeled diagrams, maps, chart completions.* Like sentence completions, these require legible handwriting and adequate space. But they are less ambiguous than sentence completions. Variations are

- Fill-ins for Harvard outlines

- Fill-ins for other kinds of graphic organizers

- Fill-ins for timelines

♦ *Putting items in order.* This works well for tests in literature and history, where a knowledgeable person could be expected to know the order of events. It also works for science and math, where the knowing the order of process steps can be part of assessment.

♦ *Constructed response.* Constructed response questions usually require complete sentences or full essays. When evaluating these, we should separate content area from writing skills as much as possible, realizing that the ability to communicate in a subject is an essential part of what we are assessing for. Some teachers require proper spelling only in subject area terms. (Actually, insisting on proper spelling of terminology is more important than just cosmetic, as spelling yields clues to meaning and related terms. Also, proper spelling lends credibility to the writer. We might feel a bit uneasy going to a *pharmacist* who calls himself a *farmasist*, or riding across a bridge designed by a self-styled *enjineer*.)

Constructed responses need not be in sentence form. They can be full show-your-work math problems, or other displays that might be appropriate for science classes.

Follow-Up on Wrong Answers

Going over the correct answers on a multiple choice testing class has little value. Students tend to pay little attention to what would matter most, which is how their logic went awry. If information on the multiple choice test was worth learning for the test, then it should be important enough to warrant some follow-up. The follow-up could be on the information itself, or it could be on the logic necessary to figure out the answer to the question.

Let's consider three kinds of multiple choice tests:

♦ *Homework checks.* Did the students gather certain information and file it in their brains? This kind of test is usually given after a reading assignment.

♦ *Information checks.* Did the student learn a set of facts? This kind of test is similar to the homework check, but it includes information learned in class as well.

To follow up on the above two tests, the students would simply have to produce the correct answer, but they should take that a step further to staple the information onto their brains. You might ask them to write a sentence expressing the information that they didn't know on the test, or construct some kind of chart, list, or set of notes.

♦ *Reading comprehension for critical understanding.* When students have wrong answers on this kind of test, which calls for making inferences and interpretations, they really should be guided to an activity which will improve their logic and reading skills.

Here is a follow-up that I use for the kind of reading comprehension that would appear on a State Assessment, SAT, or Advanced Placement test:

The students get their graded papers back. They can then earn back points by analyzing their incorrect answers. I give them the answer sheet. They can earn back a certain number of points on each item, depending on how complete and sensible their analysis is, using the format in Figure 7.3.

Figure 7.3. SAT Questions Chart

Question #	What I was thinking...	What I should have been thinking...

The student may find that she misread a pronoun reference or misinterpreted syntactical clues. This kind of reading error is extremely common in subject area tests because multiple choice question stems, as well as the passages themselves, usually are expressed with complex syntax. Complex syntax uses lots of pronouns and the reader needs to link them to the nouns that they represent. Complex syntax also demands that a lot of information be kept in short-term memory before the full meaning of the sentence is revealed. And complex syntax demands that readers process relationships within the sentence, relationships that are hooked together by relative and embedded clauses. In other words, the student who has lost meaning in text, has to go back an untangle some of the wiring of the sentence.

The student may find that she didn't know, or improperly interpreted a key word in the text or in the question.

Or, she may have been tripped up by the format of the question. Questions that ask for negatives can be tricky. These are sometimes phrased as "All of the following are true except…" or "Which of the following is not…" Another question format that can be troublesome asks students to identify more than one correct statement from a given set.

Another common error in test-taking occurs when the student reads only part of the question stem. The answer chosen correctly applies to only part of the question stem. This student needs to slow down and attend more closely to the language of the question.

In doing this kind of postmortem analysis, students may learn valuable, idiosyncratic test-taking strategies.

Conclusion

You might want to compose tests in high-reading and low-reading versions. The low-reading versions would be heavy on the single-word questions, and they might contain more visual assists. Some teachers vary the number of questions to accommodate students who are significantly affected by time constraints.

I gave a workshop once where an administrator asked me what I thought about test alterations where fewer multiple choices would be offered for struggling students. I had never heard of this before. I think there are better ways to accommodate needs. Making a test easier for some students, while others work at the standard version, seems condescending to the struggling learners and unfair to everyone else. Differentiated tests should be constructed so that the rigor for everyone is the same, although the means of accessing information is adjusted to the learner's style.

In giving you these suggestions for differentiating traditional tests, I'm assuming that you want every student to demonstrate understanding of the same body of knowledge.

8

E-Communications

This chapter will walk you through the various kind of e-communications and explain their instructional uses. I am dividing e-communications into three arenas:

♦ Whole-class communications

♦ Intraclass communications

♦ Teacher–student communications

You, of course, know that student-to-world communications are also possible and popular. Although student-to-world communications offer many educational benefits, I'm not promoting them for classroom use because of the dangers inherent in having young people communicate directly with strangers.

I. Whole-Class Communications (Teacher-to-Whole Class)

Most of the class Web sites that I've seen are online information boards. Although this is handy, and although many teachers have done a commendable job of making their sites inviting spaces for students to visit, a class Web site can function as much more than a virtual bulletin board.

I use my class Web site for three purposes:

♦ Information center

♦ Classroom library

♦ Prescriptive lesson center

My class Web site is located at www.myschoolonline.com. This one of many hosting services that offer an unlimited number of pages to teachers at a reasonable annual rate and with no advertising. I have another site on TeacherWeb, which is a little less expensive, but more sophisticated and not as simple as myschoolonline.com to use. Many districts offer Web-site-hosting service directly, but doing such a service is not without its problems. Sites maintained by teachers on district space are then the responsibility of the district, along with any errors or lapses in judgment that inevitably occur. My district does not offer space for class sites, so I've chosen to purchase space on my own.

1. *Information center*. I post to the site on a weekly basis, faithfully. It operates as Command Central for my classes. This takes some work, but it saves class time. Students know that on the site is homework, due dates for readings, what to expect for the upcoming week. Absentees are expected to consult the site to find out what they've missed. Parents can find out what expectations are in advance, which is a lot better than the phone call telling them what their child has not handed in. In short, the Web site is an efficient communicator for all concerned.

2. *Classroom library*. My site links to a variety of enrichment materials, forming a virtual library. Although I pay for myschoolonline.com out of my personal funds, when I think of how much out-of-pocket money I've spent over the years building up my classroom bookshelves, I know it's a good investment. The temptation is to overdo it, providing far more links than would ever be used by the students. A better use of the site is to have just a small but targeted array of links that students might actually look at and that I can refer to as I teach. The links are for remediation, review, and advancement. I compose hotlists for specific assignments.

3. *Prescriptive lesson center*. I have posted to my site a collection of targeted lessons that students need to improve their writing skills in very specific areas. When I read a student's paper, I direct them to one of these lessons by writing Rx, and the name of the skill, on the top of their paper. To learn how prescriptive lessons work on a school-wide basis to improve writing in all subject areas, see the description of RxWrite, RxRead, and RxResearch in Chapter 9, Prescriptives.

Mrs. Benjamin's Site - Microso

File   Edit   View   Favorites   Tools   Help

← Back ▼   ⟳ ⬆ ⌂   ⚲ Search   ⁎⌋ Favorites   ⏥ Media   ⟳   ⊒▼ ⟲ ⊒ ▼ ⊒

Address ⓔ http://myschoolonline.com/site/0,1876,5813-154891-4-33049,00.html   ▼   ⟳ Go   Links ᐥ ⚘ ▼ Norton Ant

⊙ myschoolonline   🏠   ❔
                                                                     Home   Help

◉ Visit another site   **Mrs. Benjamin's Site**

Home Page

Reading Calendar   # Mrs. Benjamin's Classes at Hen Hud

All ClassesThis Week

Socratic Questioning

Mythology

Sports and Society   Mrs. Benjamin's Office Hours:
                                            2:25-3:15 and by appointment
Huck Finn   September: Tuesday, September 14, 21
Solace of Open
Spaces   October: Tuesday, October 12, 19
RxResearch   November: Tuesday, November 9.16
                         December: Tuesday, December 7, 14
Dialectical Journal

Dialectical Journal
Links

Helpful Links for A.P.

Strunk and White

The Things They   🗋   **What You Need to Read and When**
Carried
                         Keep up with your readings by checking this calendar frequently.
English 9 Honors

Semantics &
Rhetoric   🗋   **What's happening this week in my English Class?**
AP Language   Plans and Expectations for:
Course   Semantics
                         AP Language
Step UP on SOAPS   9Honors

Rx

StepUP on the   🗋   **Principles of Socratic questioning**
Rubric
✏ Sign up to help with   Socrates taught by asking probing questions that he pretended not to know the answers to.
  this site

                         🗋   **Mythology**
✦ Nominate this site for
  the Showcase   You need to read all of the Mythology book by January 20. Below is a study guide. If you want, you can bring handwritten notes

                         to the test.

                         🗋   **Documented Essay on Sports and Society**
                         Your documented essay on a sports and society issue is due on December 1. Every Friday, I want you to e-mail me with

                         progress on this paper, as follows:

                         🗋   **Understanding the themes in Huck Finn**
                         Check out these sites for furthering your understanding of the novel.

                         🗋   **Wyoming**
                         Here are some visuals to help you picture Wyoming while you read "Solace of Open Spaces"

                         🗋   **How to write a research paper**
                         Writing a research paper is a matter of organization and time management!

↙ Back ▾   ⏸ ⏹ ⏺   🔍Search ⭐Favorites 🎬Media 🌐 📰▾ 📄 📧 ▾ 📄

Address 🔲 http://myschoolonline.com/folder/0,1872,5813-154891-4-70260,00.html   ▾ 🔗Go Links » 🔻 ▾ Norton AntiVirus 🔲

(·)myschoolonline   🏠 | ❓
                                                                   Home | Help

◀ Visit another site   **Mrs. Benjamin's Site**

Home Page

Reading Calendar   You need to work on the skill indicated on your paper.

All ClassesThis Week

Socratic Questioning

Mythology   🗋 **Learn to use the active voice.**

Sports and Society   Active voice is more lively than passive voice.

Huck Finn

Solace of Open Spaces   🗋 **Write with colons**

RxResearch   Colons add sophistication and power to your sentences.

Dialectical Journal   🗋 **Let's get rid of some of those commas!**

Dialectical Journal Links   Nothing trips up a reader more than the unnecessary comma. A comma causes the reader to pause. If the reader

Helpful Links for A.P.   pauses unnecessarily, then meaning is impeded.

Strunk and White

The Things They Carried   🗋 **Handwriting Hospital**

English 9 Honors   Here at the hospital, you will practice the 12 habits of healthful handwriting. Follow the steps, and write out each of the
                            models that the hospital staff shows you.

Semantics & Rhetoric

AP Language Course   🗋 **It's means It is; its is used for possessives**

Step UP on SOAPS   Many writers mistake "it's" for "its." Here's why.

Rx
                            🗋 **The difference between then and than**
  Active Voice
                            Then refers to time.
  Colons
                            Than is used for comparison.
  Excessive Commas

  Handwriting Hospital   🗋 **Woman is singular; women, plural**

  It's and its   Let's separate the woman from the women.

  Then/Than

  woman and women   🗋 **Here's how to use a semicolon.**

  Semicolon   A semicolon separates two closely related independent clauses.

  Basic affect-effect
                            🗋 **Learn when to use affect, when to use effect**
  Lapsing into Summary
                            Most of the time, AFFECT is the verb; EFFECT is the noun.
  Omit Unnecessary
  Wds   🗋 **How to avoid lapsing into summary**

  Thesis:Comparison   You are here because, rather than focusing on the question, you have lapsed into summary.

  Thing   🗋 **Omit Unnecessary Words**

  Legibility   Omit unnecessary words: that is one of E.B. White's key rules.

II. Intraclass Communications
(Electronic Conferencing)

When your students go home, they contact each other electronically all night, the way you used to talk on the phone like crazy when you were their age. They do talk on the phone as well, but simultaneously, they create busy communities of multiple online conversations. These are conducted through Instant Messaging and dedicated chat rooms. You can take advantage of these natural communication networks by allowing students to hand in *blogs*. Short for *web log*, a blog is a transcript of an online conversation. A 20-minute conversation will yield several pages. By reading such a transcript, you will get to see thought on paper. You will see the intermixing of the students' e-speak language with the academic language that they've learned in your class. You'll see explorations of questions that transcend class discussion. You'll see students who rarely speak up in class come alive. There's something about the writer's self that is more revealing than the in-person self. Online communication is an emergent form of communication, a cross between writing and speech. Like writing, it uses written language to communicate, and so you may think of it as writing. However, unlike traditional writing modes, online communications do have the back-and-forth of a spoken conversation. Traditional letter writing is more of an exchange of monologues. The letter writer is uninterrupted, and must wait a considerable interval of time before receiving a response. Online messaging is literally speech in written form. Its conventions differ markedly from those of traditional writing. In fact, if you were to enter an e-conversation using the same level of formality that you apply to traditional writing, you would mark yourself as an outsider to the speech community. You need to be taught the conventions of e-speak—its abbreviations, acronyms, and figures of speech. It's the speech and informality of e-speak that give it its exuberance. If you decide to widen your classroom communications in this way, you need to accept e-speak communications. To impose the conventions of formal edited English on an e-speak conversations would be as inappropriate as requiring linen napkins and fine silver at a picnic table.

Students can select partners with whom to establish a conversation online. They can do this at home, during study halls, or during class. You can rotate groups of students to computer clusters to have their discussions, or you can go to the computer lab as a class. The discussion community can be as small as two people or as large as the whole class, but smaller discussion groups are going to be more interesting. You can reconvene the class and exchange blogs between groups. Students can annotate the blogs, analyze them, or use them as a basis for further discussion or as a prewriting activity.

An electronic conversation that responds to a given prompt is called a threaded discussions interactive study guides, review sessions, and extensions of issues raised in class. You can run these sessions yourself in class (as a class) or you can assign students leadership roles in running such sessions.

Blogging and threaded discussions constitute differentiated instruction of process because not everyone's conversation is going to look the same. The questions that base them should be open ended or process oriented. Here are some suggestions for using e-communications in the learning process:

- *Avoid concrete, workbook-like questions.* Instead, favor complex questions that require interpretation, processing, synthesis, and risk-taking.

- *Don't feel the need to evaluate every conversation.* Trust the inherent value in having students converse about a thought-provoking question.

- *Resist the teacherly urge to correct the English.* Show enthusiasm for expanding your own language by learning the conventions of e-speak.

III. Teacher–Student Communications (e-mail)

E-mail can be used to collect student work and answer questions.

The advantages of collecting written work by e-mail are several. First of all, you eliminate the time wasted in class collecting and arranging papers. Second, you may find it easier to respond to student work onscreen, using the comments feature from the Insert menu. If like me, you prefer onscreen reading and writing to paperwork. You can return papers online, or on a disk, or by printing it out in school. You may feel uneasy at first, and disorganized. I suggest the following:

- Make e-mail submissions an option, rather than a requirement.

- Ask for the work to be sent in an attachment, rather than as part of an e-mail message.

- Acknowledge receipt after you've filed the work on a disk or CD.

- Remind students that e-communications can, like paper, get lost. They need to save their work.

- Be patient and flexible with this new system.

As for answering student's questions via e-mail, you may or may not feel comfortable doing this when you are at home. You may open your preparation period to student e-mail questions a few days a week. If you are comfortable with this method of communicating to students, you may find it surprisingly rewarding. Some people are better communicators in writing than they are face to face. You may have students who ask interesting questions and make fine observations to you in writing that you'd never see in a classroom.

Active Rehearsal

Active rehearsal is the process through which the learner comes to "own" the information and skills. Something that the learner does, beyond just passively receiving information through speech or the written word, integrates the new information into the learner's life. Active rehearsal can take many forms. As an effective teacher, you want what you teach to become a part of the students' lives, more than just answers on a test. For that to happen, the words have to be put into the students' mouths and hands. Communication is an important one of them. E-communication is not a replacement for face-to-face communications. Used well, it will enhance a student's confidence and lead to connections that will make the learning last.

Disadvantages of E-Communications

The disadvantages of bringing e-communication into your teaching world are more to you than to your students. They can only benefit. However, if your are not careful, you will find your workday extended in a way that threatens to overtake your life, a life already infringed on by out-of-class demands. You need to set limits and nurture a well-developed life outside of work. It's easy to allow e-communications to pile up in volumes that you can't handle. Establish guidelines as to what you are going to read thoroughly, and what is simply process work. Process work does not have to be evaluated.

I've mentioned that the writer's self differs from the physical self. Because of this, students may extend their communications to you in ways that could be misinterpreted if taken out of context. Keep e-mail communications within professional borderlines. Use the e-mail address that you use for professional, not personal, matters. Don't give students access to your personal e-mail address. Don't accept Instant Messages from students.

Any change takes adjustment. Eventually, you'll find procedures that work for you. Remind your students to carefully label their e-mail attachments with their names, rather than just naming them "My Essay."

Consider the needs of students who don't have access to technology at home. Help these students find access at the public library or at school. Students without access at home are the very ones who need technology the most, so you wouldn't be doing them a favor by excusing them. On the other hand, you can't expect them to do with technology what students with home access can do. Another problem is that not all parents approve of their children using the Internet at all. You may need to have assuring conversations with these parents. Be prepared to compromise and offer alternatives.

Just as you need to guard against letting the job encroach on your personal life more than it already does, your students are entitled to downtime. Once you get hooked on e-communications, you'll have a lot of great ideas—wonderful ways for your students to spend their evenings and weekends. Don't forget that just because more opportunities for learning are out there, they do have other interests and commitments.

And, of course, technology doesn't always work. Always have a back-up plan. A lot of what we do with technology is cooperative learning. Be sensitive to students who are new or who don't have friends in the class. For all of its advantages, most schools and communities are not ready to go "full tech" yet. Do what you can; encouraging e-communication, but offer options.

Conclusion

E-communication offers possibilities that go far beyond the on-screen bulletin boards and key pals currently in practice. It is through e-communication that your students will infuse your professional language into theirs. And, in learning more about their e-speak, you will model your own interesting lifelong education.

9

Prescriptives

We assess through observation, performance, and tests. We give feedback: commentary and/or grades. As a result, we may come to know about our students' strengths and weaknesses. Then what? Prescriptive lessons direct students to specific learning experiences that address demonstrated needs. Prescriptive lessons should not be only remedial. Students who are ready for advancement should have prescriptive lessons to move them forward as well.

This chapter will explain three Internet-based classroom structures that are the base of operations for prescriptive lessons. I call these RxWrite, RxRead, and RxResearch. These sets of prescriptive lessons are used for middle and high school classrooms in various content areas.

The classroom management for the Rx's could not be simpler: The teacher reviews the student's work and writes Rx: (name of lesson) on the student's paper. The student then does the prescribed lesson on the Web site, and turns it in either as a hard copy or electronically. If the latter, the students can either e-mail the teacher with the lesson as an attachment, or they can save their lessons in a file.

RxWrite

www.myschoolonline.com/NY/rxwrite

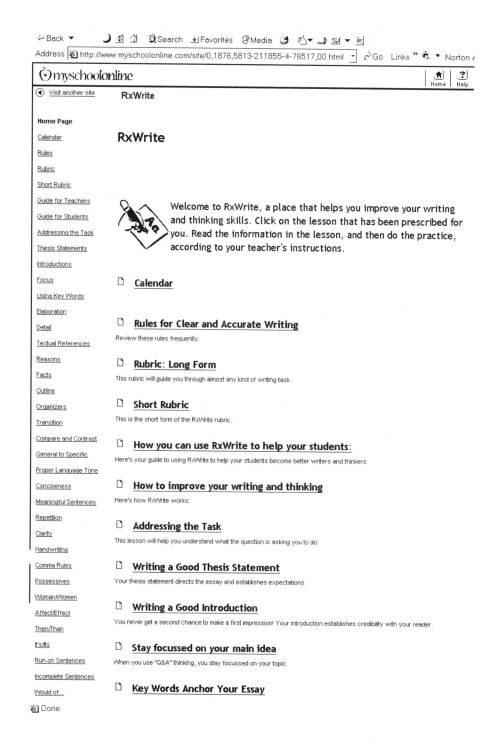

In my school, Hendrick Hudson High School, in Montrose, New York, former Principal Keith Schenker and Assistant Principal Scott Wood had the vision of improving writing performance in all subject areas. They asked me to help them brainstorm ways to achieve the following goals:

♦ Increase quality and quantity of writing tasks in all subject areas

♦ Improve student writing in terms of grammar, spelling, punctuation, and capitalization, as well as language tone, addressing the task, and coherence

♦ Establish benchmarks for writing achievement at each grade level

♦ Establish staff development to make the above three goals happen

In our brainstorming session, guided by these vision statements, we kicked the problems around a bit. Not all subject area teachers (to say the least) would have buy-in. Integrating effective writing instruction means more than just assigning essays and grading them. Yes, students need practice, but the practice must be supported with targeted instruction. Otherwise, we will keep getting back the same poor quality product, with discouraging effects. Yet, teachers of subjects other than English usually don't understand what goes into effective writing instruction. Even if they did, who has time? We can repeat the slogan that "every teacher is an English teacher," but it's a long way from saying that to making any lasting change.

The last thing I want is to ignite a controversy over who should be teaching English. The last thing I want is for colleagues to resent that they have to take up where the English department leaves off in terms of teaching writing. I do realize that writing instruction happens to be a sensitive area not only because it is an exorbitant amount of work to review essays, but also (and this is not to be minimized) many people suspect that they themselves are just a tad less than perfect when it comes to setting words onto paper and leaving them there for all the world to see. Without sensitivity to these concerns, our project is sure to fall short.

However, improving writing in all subject areas is of paramount importance. This is true now, more than ever before. Not only do standards in all subject areas, including mathematics, require writing, but also, the new SAT has a writing-on-demand component as well as a section requiring students to edit complex sentences and text. A 2003 report by the National Commission on Writing in America's Schools and Colleges opens with this statement:

> American education will never realize its potential as an engine of opportunity and economic growth until a writing revolution puts language and communication in their proper place in the classroom. Writing is how students connect the dots in their knowledge.... The nation's leaders must place writing squarely in the center of the

school agenda, and policymakers at the state and local levels must provide the resources required to improve writing

The report goes on to make a strong case for a dramatic increase in the quantity of writing that students do in school, particularly outside of English classes. Few learning activities are more comprehensive than writing. Writing helps students internalize and retain information. It's simply one of the best pedagogical investments that we can make. Hence, the RxWrite Project.

We came up with the RxWrite Project to avail students of writing instruction online. RxWrite is a collection of online, targeted lessons to which teachers in all subject areas, at all grade levels, can direct students in response to demonstrated needs. The teacher reads the writing task, which could be a social studies essay, a science lab report, an art review, a chapter summary, or any other genre of academic writing. The teacher evaluates the piece, using a generic rubric. But here's the difference: Rather than just giving the student a grade and moving on, the teacher has the option to refer the student to one of the RxWrite lessons. The student simply goes to the Web site, does the one-page prescribed lesson, and then either prints it out and hands it in, or e-mails it to the teacher.

Teachers have full discretion regarding how to use the RxWrite lessons. Some will decide to award *buy-back* points, restoring a certain number of points when the student shows competence on a particular point. Some may not collect the RxWrite lessons at all believing that the skills learned will manifest themselves in future assignments, or else not be worthy of a grade reward. Others may assign RxWrite as homework, or bonus points, or as a component of a bank of optional points.

The RxWrite lessons always refer students back to their own writing and demand revision in a targeted skill. Because the lessons are grounded in student work, the student can do the same lesson multiple times, and it is not possible for them to simply copy off someone else's work, because it is a portion of their own work that they have to rewrite. Of course, not all students (to say the least) have enough internal drive to do what is in their own best interests. Teachers need to provide incentives in both directions: Negative incentives for failure to do the prescribed RxWrite and positive incentives once they are completed.

The question of whether students may be allowed to rewrite an entire piece for a new grade is always vexing. Some teachers strongly believe in this practice. Others don't favor it, either because of the amount of time that it would take to reread student papers while another batch is pouring in, or simply because they feel that it is *they*, and not the students, who have made the corrections on the paper already. They say, "Why should you get a higher grade just because you've fixed up a few misspellings and added one sentence?" RxWrite does not ask for a rewrite of an entire piece, only a portion of it, and even then, only in a targeted way.

The RxWrite lessons change periodically, showing students different models and examples. This is because it may take students several times to show improvement. Also, the kinds of lessons offered in RxWrite are generic: As the student progresses, she will have an ongoing need to improve her ability to write a strong thesis statement, for example, or to develop a piece with effective academic language.

As you'll see, the RxWrite lessons always refer the student to authentic work that is in her life right now. The need for the writing improvement addressed in the lesson is real and immediate. RxWrite lessons, because they stress the basics, can be used in middle school or high school.

Ideally, the RxWrite lessons are more than just remediations. Students ready to advance can do so through RxWrite lessons where the teacher already sees strengths and wishes the student to build on them. The advancing or remedial student does not have to know why he or she is given a particular lesson to do. If weak students see stronger students being referred to prescriptive lessons, the lessons will lose any sense of stigma that they might otherwise have if used only for remediation.

Using the RxWrite Rubric

The RxWrite rubric is available to all students as part of their student handbook. Teachers use it as they see fit, but the idea is for students and teachers to internalize the contents of the rubric. The long form lays out the range of quality on each category, but would require too much paper if everyone used it consistently. Hence, there is the short form, which can be condensed into a half a page, or even compacted even further and made into a self-sticking note or a stamp.

Going Live with RxWrite

After I wrote a draft of the RxWrite lessons, the small planning group met again to decide the best way for our school to start using it. We decided to pilot it with a small group of interested English and social studies teachers. I met with a group of four teachers, fine tuning the rubric and reviewing student writing. We talked about how each of us would refer students to RxWrite lessons, and how we would follow up. Key to the success of a program like this is that teachers have to start slowly, integrating prescriptive lessons into their own classroom management and pedagogical routines. I stressed that RxWrite is supposed to solve problems, not create them. Not all students need to be referred to lessons every time they write something.

Record keeping is important. If you were to just write Rx's on student papers without tracking who is being referred to what, you'd be confused when the responses came in. Here are some recommendations for keeping RxWrite manageable and effective:

♦ Don't assign RxWrite lessons to every student on the same writing task, unless you are prepared to receive responses for different lessons all at once. You might want to use *RxWrite* with one class at a time or assign one area of the rubric at a time.

♦ Remember that any work that students do to improve their writing in your subject area is valuable work, even if it's just a little.

RxResearch

If there's one task that students have difficulty with, it's the research paper. The research paper is a long task, riddled with arcane academic details. RxResearch is a teacher aide for the recursive process that students need to go through to produce an elementary research paper.

One of the biggest thorns in teaching the research paper is the existence of multiple style guides. Many schools have teachers who don't agree on a single style guide. RxResearch, therefore, provides links to samples of MLA, APA, and CBE styles. The *Learning Curve* links on RxResearch provide quiz-type activities intended to give students practice on the details of documentation.

http://teacherweb.com/NY/HendrickHudsonHighSchool/MrsBenjamin/index.html

Web   **RxResearch**

Learning Curve 1   **Learning Curve 2**   **Learning Curve 3**

Learning Curve 4   **Research Paper FACTS**   **Step-by-Step**

Thesis Statements   **The Citation Machine**   **Paraphrasing**

Plagiarism   **Outlining**   **20 Common Errors**

Finishing Touches   **APA and MLA Style**   **Learning Curve 5-7**

Prescriptive Lessons for Other Subjects

You might want to start a collection of Web-based lessons addressing specific concerns in another subject area. Perhaps you are a math or physics teacher, and some of your students get tangled up because they need work on the basics. Perhaps you teach Italian and your students need to understand what direct objects are. Or perhaps you teach biology and some of your students are having difficulty breaking down the terminology into prefixes, suffixes, and roots. Your Rx: Italian or Rx: Biology doesn't have to be as elaborate as what you see in RxWrite, but you can offer three or four useful lessons to start. Later, you can build with members of your department.

There are two ways to build a collection of Web-based prescriptive lessons, and you can combine them. The most expedient way (though you might not get exactly what you want) is simply to put together a Hot List through Filamentality (www.filamentality.com). Doing so is as easy as completing a form. You can select ready-made puzzles, lists, and student activity sheets from services such as Quia or Ed Helper (www.quia.com; www.edhelper.com).

The second method is to compose your own lessons. This is of course more time consuming, but has the advantage of giving you exactly what you want. I suggest that you keep the following guidelines in mind as you compose your own Web-based prescriptive lessons:

♦ *Use a writing style that speaks directly to the student.* Be explicit, simple, and clear. Get an objective opinion as to whether your directions and explanations are clear and concise.

♦ *Give the student something to do that cannot be copied.* This can be done by requiring that the students correct their own work or tests. If that is not applicable, students should be required to handwrite their responses.

♦ *Think in terms of skills, rather than content.*

♦ *Take learning styles into account.*

♦ *Be respectful and careful about your own time management and organizational systems.* Don't overwhelm yourself. Remember that not every student has to do prescriptions every time.

♦ *Require that the prescriptions be done, but give a reward, such as buy-back points, for them.*

♦ *Consider eye appeal.* The prescriptive lessons should look user friendly and inviting to students who may approach the task with a negative attitude.

◆ *Don't forget the needs of advancing students.* Prescriptive lessons should not be merely remedial in nature.

Conclusion

Just as a physician does more than give a diagnosis, teachers can compile lessons that can be used as an "academic pharmacy," where students go to find the exact lessons that they need. Prescriptive lessons allow for an organized and manageable way for students to improve targeted skills.

10

Assistives & Tutorials

Quia for Reinforcement and Review

Quia (www.quia.com) is a subscriber service which allows teachers to construct a variety of games and puzzles and to access games and puzzles on their database created by Quiz editors and members. Quia has an Instructor Zone, in which you would create or access activities, and a Student Zone, in which students access the activities that you have posted. Quia, then, acts as a file cabinet for your classroom.

One advantage of Quia is that it's a handy way to use supplemental class time, such as times when you are working with a group or when students finish early. If DI overwhelms you with its classroom management and paperwork demands, you might look to Quia as a way to keep things neat and controlled, yet productive.

Quia activities have a lot to commend them: They are strongly visual and kinesthetic. Students can work on them alone, cooperatively, or competitively. They offer possibilities for tremendous variety in subject area as well as difficulty level. Students can work on them at their own pace, and they can time themselves to improve fluency of performance in word recognition and computations.

Many people find word games fun and engaging. I like to make them, work them, and compete for speed. For those like me, Quia activities can be a boon for learning the kind of information that needs to be memorized and for doing skills such as arithmetic and spelling.

The one disadvantage of Quia activities is that they do call for short, concrete answers. That isn't really a disadvantage, as a certain amount of learning is fact-based and repetition is a valid way to learn certain facts and skills. But some people might regard Quia and similar programs as e-workbooks: mere time-passers and seatwork. Short-answer activities should not take the place of constructed responses, abstractions, and open-ended questions.

Quia offers the following activity types:

Java Games. Java games are matching, concentration, word search, and flashcards.

Given one list of words, Quia composes these four kinds of game activities. Because of the visual-memory nature of these activities, they are well suited for spelling (but be careful not to supply the wrong visual cue as a distractor).

Matching, concentration, word searches, and flashcards are for the kinds of thinking that rank low on Bloom's taxonomy, which is not to say that some students don't need them. Of the four, my least favorite is the word search, because the student spends fruitless time sifting through distracting letters and not enough time thinking about meaning. However, word searches are pretty good for spelling, as the student has to attend to the word letter by letter. If you use Java games to bring students to a basic level of identification of terms, be sure to have it as your goal to advance them to higher level thinking activities as soon as they are ready.

Quiz and Miniquiz. You can use Quia to make or refer students to existing self-correcting, short answer quizzes. Some of the existing quizzes contain constructed responses, which are not self correcting. The Quia quizzes are great for students who are capable of independent review. Students whose parents are able to help them at home benefit from this resource.

You can create quizzes easily with all kinds of visual templates provided by Quia.

Battleship. Quia allows you to set up three levels of difficulty for the Battleship game. In my Instructor Zone, I have set up a few Battleship games about terminology for U.S. Government.

http://www.quia.com/ba/1112.html	
The Government of the United States: BASIC LEVEL	http://www.quia.com/ba/1105.html
The Government of the United States: INTERMEDIATE LEVEL	http://www.quia.com/ba/1111.html

Challenge Boards. Challenge Boards allow for one or two players. Students can choose questions worth varying amounts of points, not necessarily awarded for difficulty.

Columns. The Columns activity can be set up as matching columns. A flexible feature is that you don't need the same number of items on both columns. This means you can set up a true/false activity simply by using *true* and *false* as items on the right hand column. You can also set up a Columns activity which calls for categorization: Write the *examples* in scrambled order on the left hand column; the *categories* on the right.

Cloze. Cloze is a reading comprehension activity in which the reader supplies missing words in the text. Cloze activities do test for reading comprehension; but they also strengthen reading abilities because they force the reader to concentrate and apply critical thinking skills about what words would make sense in context. In Quia's Cloze activities, the reader is given multiple choices for the omitted words. Quia shows you exactly how to create the Cloze activity from imported text.

Jumbled Words. In the Jumbled Words activity, students just have to unscramble words. This activity is appropriate for spelling because the student has to attend to each letter.

Hangman. This is the familiar letter-by-letter game. Students enjoy it, and it does have value in reviewing terminology and spelling. It should be used as one of the Quia choices, but in terms of its value in promoting high level thinking, Hangman is one of the more limiting activities.

Patterns. In the Patterns activity, the student supplies information from a multiple choice list. If the student gets all five items in the pattern correctly answered, an image of a coin appears. The denomination of the coin increases as the student completes each set of patterns.

I like the Patterns activity for information such as verb conjugations, spelling, or any set of information that comes in a series, such as math computations. It's probably best used for remediation and review, where the student has unlimited time to build capacity in the kinds of mental activities that need to become automatic. The Patterns activity is great for students with distractibility problems, because the screen is very plain.

Picture Perfect.

Words with prefixes	http://www.quia.com/pp/23315.html

In Picture Perfect, you uncover a hidden picture as you match items on a playing board. The activity above has students alphabetizing a list of prefixed words to uncover a picture of the *Mona Lisa*. This activity is appropriate for students who, despite being in the middle grades, need to spend time attending to words letter by letter and who still need work in word analysis.

Below are two links to Picture Perfect math processes:

http://www.quia.com/pp/23318.html	3
Solving quadratic equations by completing the square	http://www.quia.com/pp/23317.html

Pop-Ups. Pop-Ups are simply multiple choice questions in which the choices come up on a pop-up button.

Rags to Riches.

Easy Algebra Equations	http://www.quia.com/rr/51684.html

Rags to Riches presents answers to factual questions in multiple choice format, making it perfect as a test review device. It can also be used for math problems. I would not recommend Rags to Riches for spelling: Presenting misspelled words as choices is a poor idea, because the viewer receives the wrong visual cue.

Ordered List.

Scientific Method	http://www.quia.com/rd/21985.html

In the Ordered List activity, the student has to put events or numbers in order within a given time period. It's great for math facts, alphabetizing, and organizing timelines. It's also possible to use the Ordered List for geography: Given 20 locations, the student orders them from East to West, or North to South.

The Ordered List activity is particularly demanding when used for numerical information. The student has to operate numbers on two planes: She has to do the indicated computation *plus* the ordering. Thus, the Ordered List is suited to students who can mentally manipulate more than one set of numbers simultaneously.

The items in the list can be reordered. Reordering permits the student to practice through repetition.

Scavenger Hunt.

Animals and Adaptations	http://www.quia.com/sh/16079.html

Scavenger Hunt (Figure 10.6) is like a mini WebQuest. The student is given some Web sites and some questions. It can be as simple or as sophisticated as you like. Scavenger Hunt differentiates by having students work on questions of their choice.

I would use Scavenger Hunt to familiarize students with a few Web sites that I would like them to spend time on later on.. It's also a great way to introduce odd and interesting facts aobut a topic. To give you an idea of what can be provided through Quia, here is their list of current popular activities.

11

Using Databases to Make Instructional Decisions

We think of using technology to differentiate instruction in terms of what students can do with technology. Another arena to be discussed in this chapter is the use of sophisticated data warehouse information to guide teachers in decisions about how to find students where they are and take them to where they need to be. A *data warehouse* is a centralized collection of statistical information about students. I may include standardized test scores, report card grades, local final exam grades, and demographic data. Data warehousing is a complex and technical field involving lots of metaphorical jargon, such as *data cleansing, cubes and cube browsers, data archeology, ECTL processes*, and others. I mention this because it's easy to feel overwhelmed by the language of data warehousing, as if we don't already have enough new things to learn as teachers.

My goal is not to lead you down the path that only psychometricians tread. Rather, I just want to show you how you be what is called the *end user*. That is, I'd like to show you how a database can inform your decisions as you group students, work with special education teachers, make recommendations for class placements, and judge whether students have improved their knowledge in measurable ways.

To begin, here is a basic lexicon for discussions about databases. This information comes from *Designing and Using Databases for School Improvement*, by Victoria L. Bernhardt (2000), which contains detailed, but accessible, information for administrators wishing to establish a data warehouse and train personnel in its use.

Terminology

Aggregate: The combination of results of all groups comprising a given population. The opposite of *aggregate* is *individual*.

Authentic assessments: These are a variety of ways to evaluate a student's demonstration of knowledge and skills, *not* including traditional or standardized testing. Examples of *authentic assessments* are projects, performances, exhibitions, portfolios, and other demonstrations of knowledge that may be assessed on a rubric or assessed holistically, but that do not lend themselves to comparative, objective measurement in the same way as a standardized, criterion-referenced, or norm-referenced test. Although we value authentic assessments, the results of these are usually not included in a data warehouse.

Cohort: A *cohort* is a particular group of individuals, such as members of a given class. A longitudinal study would be one that follows a cohort through the grade levels. A *matched cohort study* would compare, let's say, the class of 2010 of your school district with that of another district having a similar demographic. An unmatched cohort study would be one that looks just at a given cohort for your school, without comparing it to that of another school.

Criterion-referenced tests: These are tests whose items are judged in relation to a particular objective standard. In a *criterion-referenced test*, a student's score is not compared to that of other students.

Data mining: These are techniques of digging into the data to find patterns and to pull out specific kinds of information from a large database.

Data warehouse: This is the structure that supports the collected data and provides the means to locate information.

Database: This is a storage mechanism for data. In a *database*, information is entered once, and then the database has the technological capability of distributing it so that it can be used in various programs for various purposes.

Demographics: Statistical information about a population, such as average age, number of students in a school, percentages of ethnicities, socioeconomic information, gender, and other relevant information about the kinds of people that make up the population.

Disaggregate (verb): To *disaggregate* data is to separate it out into groups, such as by gender or by students who have had particular kinds of training.

Drill-down (noun) or drill down (verb): A *drill-down* is a process in which you would dig into the database in search of increasingly detailed information. For example, if you wanted to know how many students in your fifth-period biology class passed the standardized reading comprehension test last year, you would drill down until you extracted that information. The opposite process, *drill-up*, would go from the specific to the general. You would drill up to determine if a particular student's performance on your midterm exam comports with that of his cohort on a multitude of standardized tests taken over the past three years.

Frequency distribution: A frequency distribution will show you how often a given score appears. Frequency distribution will help you group students and spot trends and anomalies.

Gain score: This is the change of difference between two sittings of the same person or cohort in the same test. Despite the word *gain*, a gain score is not necessarily positive. If students did worse on a test the second time they took it, that would give you a negative gain score.

Grade-level equivalent: These are expressed in terms of the year and month of a school year, based on an average of how students at that level perform. Scores would be noted, for example, as 7.5, meaning the fifth month of the seventh grade.

Mean: The average score in a set of scores, calculated by adding up the scores and dividing by the number of scores. Most teachers are accustomed to assigning report card grades based on calculation of a mean, with some grades counting more heavily than others.

Median: The score that falls right in the middle of the distribution, 50% being higher than the median, and 50% being lower. If the number of scores is even, then the *median* is calculated by finding the mean of the two contiguous middle scores.

Mode: The most frequently-occurring score in the distribution.

Normal distribution: Also known as a *normal curve*, or famous *bell curve*, this is the bell-shaped distribution of scores, with the bulk of the scores falling in the middle.

Norm-referenced tests: These are tests in which the scores are compared to a particular group, called the norm group. The *norm group* is a representative sample of a population. Norms are determined by representative scores of a given group of test takers.

Percentile rank: These are percentages of students in a norm group, such as a national or local group of test takers, who fall below a give score. A student whose percentile rank is 70% would have scored higher than 70% of the test takers.

Query: Your request for information into the database is called a *query*. Your ability to use the database will depend on your skill at making queries.

Raw scores versus scaled scores: The *raw score* is simply the number correct (or incorrect) on the test. The *scaled score* is the conversion of that score into some sort of mathematical formula. You are already used to scaling scores when you figure out how much each item counts to get a score based on 100 points. Scores can also be scaled on the basis of a curve or a scale other than 100 points.

Now you have a very basic language for comprehending data to make decisions in your class as to how you will differentiate instruction. Put into practice, this language may look like the following cases.

Case 1: Using the Database
to Make Decisions About In-Class Grouping

Andrea Elliot teaches eighth-grade social studies. Her students are learning the structures and branches of American government. She wants to divide the class into six groups of four. Each group will answer questions based on case studies in Constitutional law. Andrea wants the groups to be balanced in terms of academic abilities and attitudes. She can observe attitudes herself, but she wants her decisions about academic ability to be informed by reading scores, past performance in social studies and English. Using the school's data warehouse, Andrea queries the database for norm-referenced test scores in reading comprehension. She assembles her groups, seeing to it that every group has at least one student scoring in the 75th percentile or higher, and at least one student scoring below the 40th percentile. Of course, her class does not break evenly. She uses report card grades as additional information to form the groups. Each person in the group has a role: one person who takes notes, one person who organizes the notes into a PowerPoint presentation, and two people who give the report to the class. The highest and lowest scoring students are the ones assigned to giving the report to the class.

Case 2: Using a Variety of Statistical Methods
to Compute Quarterly Grades

Grant Lehman believes that his ninth-grade math students' grades in a heterogeneous class should fall into a normal distribution. In his school, top math students are placed in accelerated math classes. Grant scales his test scores so that the scores fall out in a normal distribution as much as possible. If the raw score is skewed, he curves the grades and then retests, adjusting the questions according to what the raw scores tell him that his students need to relearn or how they are ready to advance. Grant finds that because math learning is cumulative, the mean is not a reliable descriptor of what a student knows at the end of the quarter. Grant's students compute their own grades, using either the mean, median, mode, or mean of all three statistics. They also have to represent their grades in various visual formats plotted on a graph, bar graph, and pie chart.

Case 3: Using the Database
to Determine Readability of Historical Documents

Tress McCleod teaches 10th-grade social studies. Her students need to write DBQs (document-based questions). To do this, she needs to provide authentic historical documents (primary documents). Some of these are public announcements, political cartoons, and visual information; but others use archaic diction with complex sentence structure. Tress wants to establish the degree to which reading deficits account for her students' difficulties in writing coherent answers to the DBQs. She asks the reading specialist to give her a readability rating of a particular document. As she suspected, the document is at a very high reading level. Tress obtains reading scores of seven special education students in her collaborative class. She and her collaborating special education teacher want the students to read the authentic documents, as they will have to do for the state exam, but right now they need assistance. The special education teacher provides a glossary for the troublesome terms and a large-print version, making the document look more reader friendly. The special education teacher provides an alternate version of the document in which she has broken down the long sentences into shorter sentences, without changing the language itself significantly.

Case 4: Using Standardized Test Scores to Counsel Students About Class Placement

Patton Andrews teaches AP English Language and Composition. His school has an open enrollment policy for AP classes, but Patton has many students for whom the AP syllabus is just too abstract. Every year, a significant number of students decide to leave AP early in the year. Sometimes, students who are not doing well are resentful of Patton, blaming him for their disappointing performance. Patton has found general correlation between SAT and ACT verbal scores and the ability to handle AP level work. This information has fortified his position when counseling students to take less demanding English courses.

Some students are simply overextending themselves by taking multiple AP courses. Patton has done a frequency distribution study, disaggregating the data to compare students with certain SAT and ACT scores who are taking just *one* AP course to those taking two, three, four, and even five courses simultaneously. These data have yielded an accurate predictor of success in AP courses.

From Data to Decisions

Bernhardt proposes the following four general data analysis categories:

1. *Overview*: How well are we doing?

2. *Examination*: Are all students succeeding?

3. *Prediction*: Can we identify students who are at risk of failing?

4. *Prevention*: What do we need to do differently?

For the classroom teacher, the most relevant information determines whether there is an unexplainable gap between a student's potential, as measured by standardized tests, and her performance. Examination of past report cards (classroom performance) will indicate whether underperformance is a pattern for a particular student. Suitable interventions can then be considered.

In the high school where I teach, the part of the data warehouse that would be of interest to teachers is accessible in the form of a large binder. Each student's data appears on a separate page. I can look up information about a particular student to determine if there is a gap between that student's performance in my class and her history. However, if I want to look at aggregate data, I need to request reports from various professionals who have been trained to drill down or drill up from the full data warehouse.

Data are useful only when we use it to find out what we should do differently to improve aggregate and individual performance. As classroom teachers, we are using multiple measures to determine student needs. These multiple measures include criterion and norm-referenced tests as well as observations, authentic assessments, and conversations with other professionals.

Elementary teachers have fewer students and are expected to know more about them and address their individual needs more than secondary students. For secondary teachers, data analysis is largely left for students in danger of failing courses or state exams and special education students.

Process Analysis

Bernhardt reminds us that "if we want different results, we must change the processes that bring about those results. We cannot continue to do the same things over and over and expect different results" (Bernhardt, 2002). This leads us to the importance of process analysis. As a classroom teacher, you should be looking at the relationship between your processes (what you are doing) and your results (assessments). Do some students need a different textbook? Do they need a different kind of reading instruction? Is the lecture and note-taking routine of information delivery working for them? Too often, we decide to give students more of the same thing that has not worked. Then we are surprised at the poor result.

Let's work with a case where eighth-grade writing results on a standardized tests in a middle school are increasingly losing ground. How will process analysis help us forge an effective improvement plan? First, analyze the data for students who are succeeding. What demographic information do we know about these students? What relevant demographics, such as socioeconomic factors, are out of our control? How much do these socioeconomic demographics account for differences between successful and unsuccessful students?

Have any of our successful students benefited from interventions, or have they always been successful? What have been the results of our interventions? This is the point at which we will find that our interventions have not had an effect. This is the point where we need to change our interventions. Change the process.

Conclusion

Data warehouses make it possible to understand student learning profiles. These understandings inform placement, expectations, remedial needs, and district-wide progress.

12

Models

In this part of the book, you will find a variety of lesson models for secondary classrooms, and how they can be enriched by technology. Most of these lessons are interdisciplinary, involve reading, and call for critical thinking.

Model 1: Research Paper:
Sports and Society

The Learning Context

Mr. Marsh teaches a college prep elective called *Social Issues*. The course is targeted to 11th and 12th graders who may have some difficulties in a competitive four-year college, and who need to integrate study skills (reading, writing, research, and time management) into the content areas.

Mr. Marsh's class is mixed, but many of these students have a negative attitude toward academics, even though most are headed to college. His goal is to equip them with the habits of mind that will ease that transition, giving them the confidence they need to carry an academic task through to conclusion without a major breakdown. He uses the newspaper and Internet heavily, trying to interest students in controversies about science and technology, censorship, privacy, civic rights, responsibilities affecting young people, and issues surrounding cars. He tries to interest students in the *New York Times* and other scholarly publications, but he's satisfied when they read popular weekly news magazines.

Mr. Marsh has recently become aware of the importance of graphic information as it relates to reading factual material. He is trying to get his students to integrate information found in graphics with narrative information: "Go from the picture to the words, from the words to the picture." Because sports is a topic involving numbers, graphs, and charts, this topic seemed to lend itself to learning from a multiplicity of information sources.

Directions to the Students:

You will write a research paper of five to seven pages that answers *your own question* about some aspect of sports in society. You may consider the following ideas:

- Athletes as heroes and role models
- Fame issues
- Sportsmanship issues
- Economic influences of sports
- Sports and racial issues
- Student athlete issues
- Young athletes and parents
- Sports and gender issues
- Violence in sports
- Sports, records, and statistics
- Sports and language
- Sports and medicine
- Sports and technology
- Sports reporting

Your central question should meet the following criteria:

- You don't already know the answer.
- The answer is complicated.
- The question is researchable.
- The question is significant and worth knowing about.
- The question will take five to seven pages to discuss.
- The question requires several different sources of information.
- The answer will combine fact and opinion.

Components of Your Paper

Abstract: You paper should open with an abstract, labeled as such. An abstract is a one paragraph summary of your purpose and findings.

Outline: This should be handed in as a separate piece. The outline is a working document. That is to say, you need an outline before you begin, but it may change as you proceed. You should find yourself going back and forth with your outline as you proceed.

The following components should be worked into your paper, in an order that you decide

- *Anecdote*: A little story involving a real person.

- *Analysis of statistics*: Your paper should contain at least one chart or graph of statistics. This material should be cited, the same as a quotation would be. You should include an analysis and/or commentary of this information.

- *Description*: At some point, you should have a descriptive paragraph, consisting of visual detail. This can be part of your anecdote.

- *Extended definition*: An extended definition is an explanation of a key concept. It differs from a dictionary definition because it operates in your particular context. For example, if you are writing about *gender equity*, you should explain what that means.

- *Block quotation*: This is a lengthy quotation (of several sentences) that is set off from the text by wider margins and single spacing. It is introduced by a colon, and followed by a parenthetical citation, unless the citation is presented in the text.

So that you are sure to include all necessary components, I want you use the comments feature from your insert menu to label the above parts. Note that they don't have to appear in this order.

At *least two sides of the issue:* This is a research paper, not a persuasive essay. Although you may express your opinion, be sure to present opposing sides as objectively as possible.

Conclusion: A paragraph at the end that sums up your paper.

Bibliography: You need at least five sources.

We will have in-class lessons on the following:

- Format/documentation techniques

- Using word processing features effectively

- Paraphrasing/plagiarizing

- Bibliography

Dates:

Monday, March 13: Submit your question.

Monday, March 20: Submit a tentative bibliography (*format doesn't have to be correct at this point*).

Monday, March 27: Submit a working outline.

Monday, April 3: Submit your abstract.

Monday, April 10: Submit two pages of the paper.

Monday, April 24: Paper is due.

Organizing Theme: The culture of sports permeates our society and offers many opportunities for reflection about issues of all kinds: economic, medical, educational, and social. By examining various issues surrounding sports, we can gain insight into ourselves as individuals, as communities, and as Americans.

Essential Questions:

♦ What are the positive and negative results of sports?

♦ What questions are raised in your mind regarding sports in society?

♦ What are the social consequences of our love affair with sports?

Assessment: Mr. Marsh will assess the final product against a rubric that the students have in advance. The rubric evaluates for the following:

Meaning. The extent to which you've done what you were asked to do.

Development. The extent to which you've provided detail: facts, figures, names, places, events, reasons, examples, and cause/effect statements.

Organization. The extent to which your reader can follow the flow of your ideas.

Language. The extent to which you've used appropriate words.

Presentation. The extent to which your paper shows respect for the conventions of the English language; the extent to which your paper is neat and carefully put together; the extent to which you've effectively used visual features to clarify your meaning for your reader (print features, graphics, font style, and headings).

In addition, Mr. Marsh keeps a check-off list for all interim work on this project. He deducts points for lateness or incompleteness on these interim assignments.

Differentiation and Technology

For this project, the teacher has used technology as an organizational tool. The tight structure of the documented research paper and the interim deadlines are not differentiated. What is differentiated is that students have a choice within the broad heading of "sports and society." This topic allows them to go back and forth between the new and the known, integrating research into their own interests, knowledge base, observation, experience, and beliefs.

Mr. Marsh teaches a modernized version of the traditional research paper. He requires students to integrate visuals with meaning. That is exactly how modern (especially young) readers read: they use textual features to help them make meaning from text. Modern writers need to keep this in mind, as they write not for themselves or for the teacher, but for other readers. Mr. Marsh clearly understands that the craft of word processing is no longer just typing, but involves a consideration of the choices available to writers about how their words should be served up to the reader on the page.

Model 2: Differentiating Math Instructing Through Instant Messaging: How Did You Get That?

Math. You can either do it or you can't, right? You're good at it or you're not.

And there's only one way to teach it, one way to learn it: The teacher goes over the homework, instructs new material, assigns homework, and that's the cycle. It works. For those for whom it works. For those that don't learn it, well… they can come for extra help, get a private tutor, or just work harder.

That *can't* be true! Eighth-grade math teacher Michelle Chavez comes to the field via special education. As a special education teacher, she has a talent for viewing math through the eyes of someone who has trouble with the traditional teacher-oriented, passive methods. When she was a student, she experienced math anxiety, especially when she had to calculate numbers under a deadline.

Michelle teaches math in a collaborative class with Justin Morrell. Michelle and Justin operate with the following tenets about how math is learned:

- ◆ Math is cumulative.

- ◆ Math must be understood, processed, and applied.

- ◆ Math learning requires the learning of a lot of new terminology. In that sense it is like learning a foreign language.

- ◆ Math has to be actively practiced every day.

- ◆ Math is more than rules and formulas.

So far, nothing new or exciting. So far, math is still a spectator sport. What elevates Michelle and Justin's math class is that they incorporate another dimension for learning math: communication.

"When I was in school, and in many classes today as well," Michelle says, "the only communication in math class is between teachers and students. Sometimes the teacher asks the questions and the students answer, sometimes the reverse, but very little *student-to-student* communication. Most of the answers are just that—answers. That's the problem. Some students need to communicate through the process. Their own communication guides them."

Michelle and Justin carefully analyzed the math process and evaluated how each stage of it could be responsive to students' needs and the use of technology.

Differentiation	*Technology*
Process Stage: Listening to Direct Instruction	
Some students need to use a stenography pad, leaving the right side clear for later review and summary notes or additional examples. Some students need to develop the metacognitive habit of putting question marks next to concepts that they are unsure of. Students who learn verbally should write both the words and the numbers. Students who are visual learners should use color-coded pens and markers.	Teachers can assist the note-taking process tremendously by using Smart Board technology. This allows the notes to be preserved. An alternative is to use transparencies or LCD projected notes or PowerPoint. Contemporary textbooks come with CDs. Most students would benefit by typing up their notes after class.
Process Stage: Reading the Math Textbook	
Struggling students need to take conscious steps to activate prior knowledge. This can by done by reviewing the previous reading material and stating its main points aloud or expressing them on paper. Students should use textual features (headings, diagrams, captions, pictures) for their intended purpose, which is to enhance reading comprehension. Understand that reading a math textbook is a unique and time-consuming reading experience. It is necessary to read recursively. Some students comprehend better when reading aloud.	Where possible, struggling students should be allowed to write in and highlight the text. Find supportive Web sites that are on the same topic. Struggling students will benefit from receiving the same information in multiple forms. Arrange for online study partners. Allow students to express their under-standings as flow charts and graphic organizers.
Process Stage: Doing Math Homework	
Set up a column on one side of the page to indicate trouble spots. Students need a process to follow when they feel defeated by the homework. The steps could be: review your notes, reread the textbook, work with a partner, say it aloud, identify your questions, and so forth.	Arrange for study partners, emphasizing process over product. Have students print out a transcript of their online conversation and then review their own thinking. If neatness is a problem, encourage the use of a word processor. Provide an online means to check answers.

Differentiation	Technology
Process Stage: Studying for the Math Test	
Students should deliberately anticipate what might be on the test. They should make up their own tests and take each other's tests. Students should understand what strengths they should capitalize on. Identify their comfort zone and trouble zones. Negative emotions can cause math blocks. Students should visualize the testing environment, repeatedly if necessary, and develop a plan for handling negative emotions, such as fear. Students should engage as many senses as possible while studying. Some people study better with music playing; others find music a distraction. Music learners should get in the habit of listening to the same music whenever they study a particular topic. When they recall that music, their memories will trigger that information. Students should practice working within the allotted time, developing a sense of how long it's going to take to do what kinds of problems.	Arrange for online study partners. Provide relevant Web sites for both practice and review of concepts. Even though the rules and formulas are readily available, students should consciously write or type them. Color coding is a powerful memory enhancer.
Process Stage: Taking the Math Test	
"Memory spill" immediately: This means, write down your formulas and rules as soon as you get your test. Students need to come into the text with strategy: do the easiest questions first; have a time management plan.	Special Education IEPs will determine the extent to which students can use technological assists during a test.

Differentiation	*Technology*
Process Stage: Getting the Math Test Back	
Make up a test analysis chart and have students self-analyze the kinds of mistakes that they made. Include these categories: • Carelessness, rushing • Carelessness, overconfidence • Misunderstanding of a main idea • Doing the wrong operation • Leaving blanks • Not knowing that this was going to be on the text • Still don't get it • Other Students need to keep their tests in an organized collection.	Here's the point at which prescriptive lessons direct the student to target lessons. If you accumulate multiple forms of a test, you might want to offer retest opportunities or buy-back points. If you have the organizational skills and patience, it's great to keep track of the kinds of mistakes and wrong answers that you are getting.

Model 3: Word-Processing Features: Autocorrect

Your word processor has an *autocorrect* feature on the tool bar. This feature already has a bank of certain commonly mistyped words, you may have noticed that it automatically edits these words for you. You can program your own abbreviations into the autocorrect options feature. Then, have your students e-mail their written work to you or hand it in on a disk. As you read the paper, you can insert your abbreviations as comments (from the insert menu) and will flip them into whatever those abbreviations stand for. Here's how it would look:

What you type in	*What autocorrect prints*
Det	Details: You need details here, such as an example, quotation, statistic, or more specific nouns.
Con	Connections: You need to make a stronger connection here. Use your list of connecting words.
Rep	Repetitive: You are being unnecessarily repetitive here. Every sentence needs to bring new information. Eliminate unnecessary words.

To differentiate, you can code the abbreviations, making them more sophisticated, like this.

What you type in	*What autocorrect prints*
Det1	Details: Give an example
Det2	Details: You need details here, such as an example, quotation, statistic, or more specific nouns.
Det3	Details: Support your assertions with specifics: textual reference, data, cases, visuals, graphics.
Con1	Connections: You need to make a stronger connection here. Use your list of connecting words.
Con2	Connections: Look more closely at how one idea leads into the next.
Con3	Segue
Rep1	Repetitive: Eliminate unnecessary words.
Rep2	Repetitive: You are being repetitive here. Every sentence needs to bring new information.
Rep3	Repetitive: The repetition of words/ideas here has no rhetorical purpose.

To get your comment to stand out in the text, you can write it in all caps, place asterisks on both sides of the comment, or distinguish it visually in some other way. You can also use the *comment* feature in the insert menu, which will set up the comment as a marginal note. You may want students to highlight your comments when you return the papers, just to assure that they have read them. Or, you could direct them to corrective lessons. In any case, students should be accountable in some way to respond to your comments.

Additional Suggestions for Autocorrect Comments

Here is a starter kit for multipurpose autocorrect comments. These apply to writing assessments in all subject areas. You might want to supplement these with specific comments for the writing that students do in your own subject.

Clar	*Clarify*: Simplify your wording so that your meaning is clear.
Fc	*Focus*: Review the question and answer it directly. Don't stray from the directions.
ParaDev	*Paragraph Development*: Put more body into this paragraph. Focus on its topic sentence.
ParDiv	*Paragraph Division*: This paragraph is too long. Build paragraphs around topic sentences.
TS	*Thesis Statement*: You need a clear and cogent thesis statement that sets forth the main idea of your paper.
Prf	*Proofreading*: Reread your work carefully.
Sent	*Sentence Sense*: Reread this sentence. It doesn't make a sensible point.
Lang:	*Language*: Use the proper, serious language for this subject area.
Org: Para	*Organization of paragraph*: Begin this paragraph with a topic sentence. Then, each sentence should flow logically from that main idea.
Org: Wh	*Organization of whole piece*: Your ideas should follow a logical and expected progression. Start with an outline.
Cap	*Capitalization*: Capitalize names of people and places on a map or calendar
Fl	*Fluency*: You have too many words or too many commas interrupting the flow of ideas.

The autocorrected student's paper might look like this:

Middle School Life Science: 7th Grade

Teacher: Karen Theodoris

Task: Compare and contrast an amphibian with a reptile in structure, reproduction, life cycle, and give examples of each.

Here's Victoria's original response:

> In my paragraph I am going to tell you about two kinds of animals and how they are alike and different. First is reptiles. Reptiles are like different kinds of snakes, turtles, alligators, crocodiles, and lizards. They are cold-blooded. Meaning they have a different temperature depending on the day outside. They have scales on there skin. They lay eggs. They live on the land. There babies look like them. The males have sperms. Now the amphibians. They have young that look not like them. They look like tad-

poles. They live on land and in the water. They don't have scales on there skin there skin is slimy. There eggs are like jellyfish in the water. They are cold-blooded.

Ms. Theodoris's assessment of Victoria's learning needs:

Victoria worked very had on this assignment. You can see that she does know the information that I asked for. I would like her to improve her sentence structure, eliminating the sentence fragments. And I'd like to see her be more organized when she writes a comparison-contrast piece. On our team, we've prioritized the comparison-contrast form. We want the students to compare and contrast two subjects concept by concept, rather than speak of them separately, as Vicky has done. And, I'd like her to get the there/their right. This is another team priority. Note: Victoria's spellchecker automatically corrected many of her words as she typed them.

Here is Victoria's paper after Ms. Theodoris has used three autocorrect comments: SEN flipped into the "incomplete sentence" comment; THER printed the their/there comment, and O translated into the "organization" comment.

In my paragraph I am going to tell you about two kinds of animals and how they are alike and different. First is reptiles.

Comment: INCOMPLETE SENTENCE: A sentence must have a subject and a verb and be able to stand alone and make sense.

Reptiles are like different kinds of snakes, turtles, alligators, crocodiles, and lizards. They are cold-blooded. Meaning they have a different temperature depending on the day outside. They have scales on there...

Comment: You've used "there" instead of "their": Remember that "their" is used to show ownership. On your correction log, write a "their" sentence and a "there" sentence.

skin. They lay eggs. They live on the land. There babies look like them. The males have sperms. Now the amphibians. They have young that look not like them. They look like tadpoles. They live on land and in the water. They don't have scales on there skin there skin is slimy. There eggs are like jellyfish in the water. They are cold-blooded.

Comment: ORGANIZATION: Which organizational plan did you use for this writing task? Select the proper organizational plan and rewrite this please.

Here's the same version, this time using the *comment* feature from the insert toolbar:

In my paragraph I am going to tell you about two kinds of animals and how they are alike and different. First is reptiles. Reptiles are like different kinds of snakes, turtles, alligators, crocodiles, and lizards. They are cold-blooded. Meaning they have a different temperature depending on the day outside. They have scales on there skin. They lay eggs. They live on the land. There babies look like them. The males have sperms. Now the amphibians. They have young that look not like them. They look like tadpoles. They live on land and in the water. They don't have scales on there skin there skin is slimy. There eggs are like jellyfish in the water. They are cold-blooded.

> **Comment:** INCOMPLETE SENTENCE: A sentence must have a subject and a verb and be able to stand alone and make sense.

> **Comment:** You've used "there" instead of "their": Remember that "their" is used to show ownership. On your correction log, write a "their" sentence and a "there" sentence.

> **Comment:** ORGANIZATION: Which organizational plan did you use for this writing task? Select the proper organizational plan and rewrite this

Other Applications of Autocorrect

Math teachers can use autocorrect comments to evaluate "show your work" math problems that are submitted electronically. In the following example, Gregory has submitted his work on a linear equation. His teacher, Cheryl McCann, has inserted comments that she has stored on autocorrect.

Gregory's work, with teacher comments:

Find the solution of set $2x–5 + 11$ if the domain is R.

$2x - 5 + 11$

$2x - 5 + 5 = 11 + 5$

> **Comment:** Alignment

$2x = 16$

$2x\ 16$

2

$x = 8$

> **Comment:** Name the solution set.

Says Cheryl, "It didn't take the kids long to learn to use the math symbols from the Insert menu. Their work is a lot more legible and accurate because they are typing it. They have to show all work, so it's the process that counts. I find that they actually do a better job on a test, when they have to work with pencil and paper. My autocorrect comments are mostly about proper use of mathematical language and procedures. They have to learn to follow the protocol. The same kinds of mistakes come up. You can predict them. I have a handful of favorites."

Mrs. McCann's math comments on autocorrect:

CALC	Check your calculations
OMIT	You've omitted a step
AL	Alignment
SOL	Include the solution set
LAB	Label all parts
Rd	Incorrect rounding
INC	Solution incomplete
SYM	Incorrect mathematical symbol used
FAC	Factoring error
REV	Reverse the order of operations
IND	Solve by indirect reasoning

Model 4: Hotlisting

In this hotlist, created on Filamentality, middle school math teacher Lisa S. Rowland creates a rich, differentiated learning experience that goes beyond the basics of a hotlist. The annotations point up the strengths of Lisa's work. The URL for this hotlist is: http://www.kn.sbc.com/wired/fil/pages/listall thinli.html

All Things Geometric: An Internet Hotlist on Geometry

Created by Lisa S. Rowland, Lowndes Middle School

- Introduction
- Vocabulary Builders
- Area, Perimeter, & the other Dimension
- The Beauty of Geometry
- Getting the Angle on Angles
- Coordinates, Tessellations, & Symmetry

Introduction

Come and discover *All Things Geometric* with the assistance of the Internet. Please remember that your assignment is to complete a minimum of two (2) *explorations* for each topic.

Comment: The teacher's language—the invitational tone and the use of the upbeat words "discover" and "explorations"—conveys her enthusiasm, promoting a positive attitude on the part of the students.

The Internet Resources

The Beauty of Geometry

Comment: These links take students to attractive sites which show them how geometric patterns function in art.

- *The Land That Design Forgot*—Ever wonder why we have to learn about geometry.... Try out this site and see how geometric ideas help Carmine redesign a playground so it works well and looks good!

- *Carmine's Introduction to Line and Shape*—Click on LINES and experience the geometry in art. When you've completed that adventure go straight to SHAPES.

- *Designing Lines*—Experiment with your own symmetrical line designs at this site. Bet you never knew intersecting lines could look so fine!

- *Polygon Maker*—Draw multi-sided spirals and nesting polygons as you experiment with design using this program.

- *Turtlechase*—Create multi-colored designs resembling string art.

- *Spider Webs*—Make your own elaborate spider webs with online string art.

- *The Art of Communicating Geometrically*—Follow the directions for these designs and then check and see if your blocks match theirs.

- *Pattern Block Design*—This is your chance to make an online design with pattern blocks and then give directions to your partner on how to duplicate it.

Vocabulary Builders

Comment: These sites use visuals and manipulatives to reinforce terminology.

- *Lines, Segments, and Rays, Oh My!*—Read about the properties of these straight objects.

- *Figures and Polygons*—Click on the names of each shape to see their picture and read about their properties. (Psst... I'd just scroll all the way down the page instead of doing all that clicking....)

- *Test Your Math: Lingo Ability in Geometry*—Check out the list of terms you should know then try your 'memory' on flashcards, concentration, a word search, or matching activities

- *... And Then There's Angle Vocab*—Check out the list of terms you should know then try your 'memory' on flashcards, concentration, a word search, or matching activities

♦ *… And Polygons and Solids…*—Caution: Read this fact sheet before clicking on the activity. This site requires more than just a definition… you must answer questions that deal with the properties of shapes.

♦ *… And a Hidden Picture to Practice Vocabulary by*—Uncover the hidden picture by clicking the picture of the vocabulary word at the bottom of the page

Getting the Angle on Angles

♦ *Types of Angles*—Explore what it means to be a complementary or a supplementary angle.

♦ *Anglin'*—This lesson will reinforce our knowledge of angles and the ways groups of angles can be related to each other: acute, right, obtuse, adjacent, and so forth.

♦ *Splat Degree*—To play this game you need to be able to estimate and use angle measures… and have our classroom username to play!

♦ *What's My Angle?*—Be sure to work through the activity section, review the fact sheet, and then try your hand with the test.

♦ *Introducing… More Angles*—Learn more about angles and parallel lines here.

♦ *The Truth about Triangles*—A triangle has three sides, but not just any set of three lengths will make a triangle. Use this linkage-strip Interactive Activity to answer questions

Area, Perimeter, and the Other Dimension

♦ *Virtual Geo-board*—Make 3 different shapes with a perimeter of 16cm then compare their areas.

♦ *Area & Perimeter—what a Pair!*—Find the area and perimeter of these shapes and see if you can discover a relationship.

♦ *What If You Wanted to Paint Your Room*—Use your knowledge of 'AREA' to design your own virtual bedroom…

♦ *Cyberchase Airline Builders*—Can you make all the different space-ships with the given material?

♦ *What's My Area: Triangle*—This lesson will help explain how to find the area of a triangle.

♦ *Pythagorean Theorem*—View the "why" of the Pythagorean Theorem with this animation.

- *What's My Area: Circle*—View the "why" of the formula for the area of a circle with this animation.

- *Introducing Volume*—This lesson will allow us to experiment with different volumes of prisms.

- 3-D *Boxes*—Determine the number of cubes needed to make these boxes…hint: remember to use the volume of a rectangular prism formula…

- *Exploring Geometric Solids*—This lesson requires a study guide. Explore the properties of geometric solids with this investigation.

- *Buried Shapes*—Identify the partially buried 3-D shapes by clicking on the correct name.

- *Dimensions*—Listen to this song entitled "Dimensions."

Coordinates, Tessellations, and Symmetry

- *Coordinate Cop*—Click on the handcuffs after you've identified the coordinates of the criminals.

- *Planet Hop*—Practice your coordinate graphing skill with this game.

- *Mine Plotting*—Practice your point plotting skills by moving a robot through a mine field in the first quadrant to a target location. Moves are accomplished by specifying the coordinates of the new location.

- *Tessellating Pattern Blocks*—Design a pattern using pattern blocks that tessellate. Then try to make the patterns according to the directions.

- *Patterns Made from Tiles*—Rotate these tiles to make your own design and then calculate the area.

- *Bathroom Tiles*—This game requires you to use your transformation skills of reflection, rotation, and translations.

- *Copycat*—Copycat is a 3-D game that requires you to duplicate a pattern that is rotating. See if you can finish the pattern with the least amount of rotations.

- *Upside down Heads*—Click on the "heads" and see the reflection they make.

Content by Lisa S. Rowland, Lrowland@lowndes..k12.ga.us, http://www.kn.sbc.com/wired/fil/pages/listallthinli.html, Last revised Mon May 24 6:42:11 US/Pacific 2004

Model 5: WebQuests: Information Adventures

WebQuests are investigative activities that are Internet-based. There are tons of excellent, peer reviewed, educator-created WebQuests at these Web sites:

www.webquest.org

www.filamentality.com

www.webquestdirect.com (a subscriber service)

www.web-n-flow.com

www.discoveryschool.com

The WebQuest idea was created by Bernie Dodge and Tom March out of San Diego State University. Kathy Schrock at Discovery School is another rich vein of information about WebQuesting.

The WebQuest paradigm improves the directions for writing a research paper. Unlike the traditional research paper, the WebQuest points the students to the sources that will yield the targeted information. When we set students loose on the Internet, we often find to our dismay that they pull up unreliable sources and flounder. When we assign a traditional resource paper, we often find to our dismay that the students complete it in a desultory manner, often plagiarizing and submitting lifeless information. But the WebQuest draws in a precise field and transforms what would otherwise be a dull task into an information adventure.

You will soon find that WebQuesting is a whole world. Right now, you can locate WebQuests on any topic you can think of and be ready to go. You can also compose your own, alter an existing WebQuest, or even assign students to create their own WebQuests. In fact, ThinkQuest is an ongoing contest for student-created WebQuests.

WebQuests have become an educational genre. As such, they have structural features:

Introduction: The introduction is an invitation to the WebQuest. It should have an upbeat, invitational tone that speaks to the student in the second person. The introduction is best when it sets up an interesting scenario and is about 100 words long. Here are some ways to begin the introduction:

Imagine that…

You are a…

Put yourself in the shoes of a…

Once upon a time…

Have you ever thought about...

Your telephone rings. It's...

_____ needs your help.

You are an expert in...

Memorandum:

The Task: Also called The Quest, the task sets forth the objective of the investigation. The language of the task should be simple and direct. Many educators include learning objectives in the task. In a sense, the task is a rubric. Like a rubric, it delineates features that the finished product should have. Be sure that this section of the WebQuest is visually clear. Use a numbered or bulleted list.

Processes and Resources: The WebQuest below goes into extensive detail in this section, dividing the experience into phases. This amount of detail may or may not be necessary, depending on the task and your students. This is where you insert your hotlist for the WebQuest. The hotlist is a collection of Internet resources that you require or suggest. You may include directions for the students to locate additional resources on their own.

Conclusion: The conclusion poses higher level questions that the students should now be able to address. Remember that WebQuesting is not about compiling facts that could be copied from a single source. WebQuesting is about problem solving, pursuing information in search of enlightenment, and examining multiple points of view. The conclusion redirects students to the learning objectives set forth in the Task.

Below is a very thorough WebQuest that immerses students into the world of the 1920s and asks them to make judgments after reading extensive information. Not all WebQuests are this comprehensive. Melnard Sebayan created this WebQuest through Filamentality. I found it by doing a Filamentality search. The topic is interesting, the task engaging, and the learning process carefully laid out for the student.

1920s Prohibition: An Internet WebQuest on Prohibition

Created by Melnard Sebayan, University of Illinois—Chicago

- Introduction
- The Process & Resources
- HyperText Dictionary
- The Task
- Conclusion

Introduction

Imagine yourself in 1920s United States. Consumption of alcohol is a way of life. Your friends and family drink alcohol and you would have a drink occasionally. The 18th amendment is then ratified. Alcohol is prohibited. You would have to decide whether to be for or against prohibition. Which side would you choose? Which is the best choice for the nation and yourself. There are different perspectives to this debate.

In the following WebQuest, you will use the power of teamwork and the abundant resources on the Internet to learn all about Prohibition. Each group will learn one piece of the puzzle or perspective and then we will come together to get a better understanding of the topic.

The Quest

Your task is to decide if the United States Government was right or wrong for passing the 18th amendment, Prohibition.

Your learning objectives for this simulation are to

- Understand the objectives of prohibition.

- Understand why the United States decided to pass the prohibition amendment.

- Understand the various perspectives on prohibition. Why people are either for or against prohibition.

- Evaluate the importance of each perspective.

- Choose one perspective and come up with the best argument for your choice.

- Understand and compare the perspectives.

The Process and Resources

In this WebQuest you will be working together with a group of students in class. You will be assigned a specific perspective to learn. Each group will answer the Task or Quest(ion). As a member of the group you will explore WebPages from people all over the world who care about Prohibition.

1. *Assign roles.* The class will be divided into 4 groups of 6 people each. One group will take the role of the 'wets'—people against prohibition. The second group will take the role of the 'drys'—people for prohibition. The third group will take the role of women, who played a significant role during prohibition. The last group will take the perspective of the breweries/producers of alcohol.

2. *Study the general background information on prohibition.* Then look at your argument or perspective. Look for the best arguments for your side. Take a bold stance. Consider the other group's argument. Find out information on the other sides. Come up with counter arguments. Finally, reassure your stance after looking at all the available information.

3. Prepare a brief written summary of your decision-making process, including your list of priorities, your list of options.

4. Each group will be given 10 minutes to present their finding and arguments to the whole class. After each group presents, we will have a 10 minute discussion. Finally, as a class we will decide the best argument, for or against prohibition.

Phase 1—Background: Something for Everyone

Use the following links to learn about the background and context of prohibition. The links below will help to answer the basic questions of who? what? where? when? why? and how? Be creative in exploring the information so that you answer these questions as fully and insightfully as you can.

Before discussing with your groups, you need to understand the following:

♦ 18th Amendment

♦ 21st Amendment

♦ The context of the 1920s (learn about the decade)

♦ Why the United States decided for prohibition and why the United States repealed prohibition.

♦ Some of the key figures and vocabulary of prohibition. Key figures will help you in your argument

• History of prohibition—key figures and vocabulary: includes links that define and discuss the key figures and vocabulary of prohibition. Example vocabulary, speakeasy, or moonshine

• Before prohibition—the practices and lifestyles that preceded the 1920s prohibition. How people previously consumed alcohol.

Prohibition Act of 1920—another history site. Discuss what the Prohibition Act of 1920 meant. Today it was known as the 'Noble experiment.'

Basic 1920s facts—good for background information on the decade. Shows the basic statistical figures of the types entertainment of this decade.

Night life—Good for information on what was happening during prohibition. What happens at night. What happened at the speakeasy and why did people go there?

The 18th Amendment—What the provisions of the amendment does. Good primary document to analyze what exactly prohibition does.

The 21st Amendment—Repeal of prohibition (primary document).

Phase 2—Looking Deeper from Different Perspectives

Instructions

- ♦ Each group will explore their assigned side or arguments.

- ♦ Read through the Web sites provided for your group. If you print out the files, underline the passages that you feel are the most important. If you look at the files on the computer, copy sections you feel are important by dragging the mouse across the passage and copying and pasting it into a word processor or other writing software.

Note: Remember to write down or copy and paste the URL of the file you take the passage from so you can quickly go back to it if you need to prove your point.

- ♦ Be prepared to focus what you've learned into one main opinion that answers the Big Quest(ion) or Task based on what you have learned from the links for your role.

You may explore other Web sites to help you!

'Wet'

'Wet' was a term used to describe the people that were against prohibition. 'Wets' included alcohol producers, people who consumed alcohol, or people who just disagreed with the idea of prohibition. They advocated that prohibition violated their liberty and freedom.

Use the Internet information below to answer these questions specifically related to 'Wet':

- ♦ How will you argue against the prohibition amendment?

- ♦ What is wrong with prohibition? Does it violate the rights of an American Citizen.

- ♦ What options did you have? Did the people either accept the law or go underground?

- ♦ Who supports your cause? Politicians? Breweries? Men? Women? etc.

♦ Consider the counter arguments to your arguments. How will the other group respond?

♦ Support your stance with hard facts and evidence.

♦ Summarize your opinions and arguments. You take one stance and that stance is AGAINST prohibition. Be ready to present and argue your stance in class.

- *Fiorella H. LaGaurdia*—New York City politician against prohibition. He argues the failures of prohibition.

- Senator Reed's testimony before the Senate.

- *Thirteen Years That Damaged America*—The negative effects that prohibition created.

- *Prohibition and the Gangsters*—The underworld's perspective. Good for information on gangsters such as Al Capone.

- *Alcohol Prohibition Was a Failure*—Secondary source for argument on why prohibition was a failure.

- *We Want Beer*—Underground and black market was very dangerous. Could an event such as the St. Valentine's Day massacre have been prevented? Argues that prohibition paved the way for the black market of beer.

'Dry'

'Dry' was term used to describe the people of the groups that favored prohibition. They wanted to clean up society by removing the vice and the vices involved with the consumption of alcohol. Use the Internet information linked below to answer these questions specifically related to 'Dry':

♦ Why did you argue for prohibition?

♦ Is prohibition morally right from your perspective?

♦ Who supports your cause?

♦ Determine your stance and find your best arguments.

♦ Consider the counter arguments to your arguments. How will the other group respond?

♦ Support your stance with hard facts and evidence.

♦ Summarize your opinions and arguments. You take one stance and that stance is FOR prohibition. Be ready to present and argue your stance in class.

- *The Churches' position*—The Churches or the religious supported prohibition. This gives their arguments in support of prohibition.

- *Local Option*—Good links for other sites. Provides an example of the idea 'local option.' This shows how individual communities dealt with the problems of alcohol.

- *Statements about Prohibition in 1928*—Primary sources. This site shows quotes from people and businesses during prohibition. The arguments for the positives created by prohibition.

- *Anti Saloon League*—Background information on the ASL. This site gives their mission statement, history, and position toward prohibition.

- *Propaganda for prohibition*—Primary sources, images, and propaganda for prohibition. Open to interpretation.

Women's Argument

Women also played a significant role during 1920s prohibition. Women were mainly for prohibition. Prohibition promoted a better lifestyle and social harmony. They favored the idea of temperance, controlling alcohol consumption. The Women's Christian Temperance Union (WCTU) played a major role also. They were the leading group crusading against alcohol.

Use the Internet information below to answer these questions specifically related to the Women's argument:

- ◆ What are your arguments?

- ◆ What was the WCTU?

- ◆ What are the things or tactics used to help their cause?

- ◆ What arguments can you offer to support your position?

- ◆ Support your stance with hard facts and evidence.

- ◆ Summarize your opinions and arguments. You take one stance and that stance is FOR prohibition. Be ready to present and argue your stance in class.

  - *Women against alcohol*—A useful Web site for the women's argument. Good source of background information on their position toward prohibition. They argue for enforcement of the prohibition law and how it is not effectively enforced.

- *WCTU*—Women Christian Temperance Union. The history of their organization. Focuses on key figures such as Francis Willard. This site also discusses what they have done and accomplished.

- *Temperance Movement*—The view and arguments toward temperance.

The Breweries

The breweries also had a major role during prohibition. Prohibition would eventually end this industry. Production of alcohol was one of the largest industries in the country. Plenty of money would be lost because of prohibition.

Use the Internet information below to answer these questions specifically related to the breweries:

- Why should we repeal prohibition—from the perspective of the breweries?

- What options do you have? Give in to the law? Protest against prohibition? Break the law?

- Does this industry loose out? Are they the biggest losers of prohibition

- Choose a stance?

- Support your argument

- Summarize your information and be ready to present your findings and opinions to the class.

Use any other Web site to help your cause.

- *Brewing Industry and Prohibition*—Shows how the Brewing industry is connected to prohibition

- *The Old Neighborhood*—The old factories continued production.

- *Moonshine*—How people ran moonshine out of their homes. The brewing industry was still booming.

Phase 3—Debating, Discussing, and Reaching Consensus

You have all learned about a different part of Prohibition. With the expertise gained by searching from one perspective, the class as a whole must now answer the Task/Quest(ion). Each group will bring a certain viewpoint to the answer: Some of you will agree and others disagree on the arguments made. Use information, pictures, movies, facts, opinions, and so forth from the WebPages you explored to convince the other groups that your viewpoint is important and should be part of your team's answer to the Task/Quest(ion). Your WebQuest team should write out an answer that everyone on the team can live with. Seek consensus among your group!

As a class we will decide if prohibition was necessary. During the 1920s, should we be for or against prohibition?

Short question: Could prohibition be applied to today?

Phase 4—Real World Feedback

You and your teammates have learned a lot by dividing up into different roles. Now's the time to put your learning into a letter you'll send out for real world feedback. Together you will write a letter that contains opinions, information, and perspectives that you've gained. Here's the process:

◆ Begin your letter with a statement of who you are and why you are writing your message to this particular person or organization.

◆ Give background information that shows you understand the topic.

State the task/quest(ion) and your group's answer.

◆ Each person in your group should write a paragraph that gives two good reasons supporting the group's opinion. Make sure to be specific in both the information (like where you got it from on the Web) and the reasoning (why the information proves your group's point).

◆ Have each person on the team proofread the message. Use correct letter format and make sure you have correctly addressed the e-mail message. Use the link below to make contact. Send your message and make sure your teacher gets a copy.

Your Contact is: _____

Conclusion

Did we make the right decision in repealing prohibition based on the perspectives we have studied? Today, there are still multiple perspectives on this topic. We still have to consider all the options and arguments available. If you're blindfolded and only 'looking' at one part, it's easy to come up with an answer that may not be completely right. It's the same for understanding a topic as broad or complex as Prohibition: when you only know part of the picture, you only know part of the picture. Now all of you know a lot more. Nice work. You should be proud of yourselves! How can you use what you've learned to see beyond the black and white of a topic and into the gray areas? What other parts of Prohibition could still be explored? Remember, learning never stops.

Content by Melnard Sebayan, msebay2@uic.edu, http://www.kn.sbc.com/wired/fil/pages/webprohibitme.html, last revised Tue Mar 9 11:03:27 US/Pacific 2004

The Bible: WebQuest Discussion Questions

The Learning Context. Mrs. Daniels' 10th-grade students have read the selections from the Old and New Testaments that appear in their literature anthology. They have read these selections aloud as a whole class. Mrs. Daniels has emphasized the poetic qualities of the literature, how its sound evokes meaning, rhythmic qualities, metaphor, and unity.

Mrs. Daniels prepared a WebQuest addressing issues of reading Biblical literature for a secular purpose. The WebQuest led to the following information:

- What is the significance of the Supreme Court's Lemon ruling? When was this ruling handed down? What are the three circumstances under which Biblical literature and religious ideas can be part of public school education?

- Find five examples of literary allusions in American or British literature. You might want to look at Shakespeare, Emily Dickinson, Herman Melville, Ernest Hemingway, or John Steinbeck.

- Define the word *epiphany*. Give examples from literature in which a character experiences epiphany.

- Many words and expressions in the English language have Biblical origins. Find 10 examples. Explain how these words or expressions are used in modern language, and how they are metaphors for a Biblical story.

Logistics

The class divided up the tasks in the WebQuest and then reported out on their information. This took two class days, one for the research and one for the reporting out.

Research, Reading, and Discussion

The main part of this lesson series has the students working in groups, doing a combination of Internet and textbook research on one of the following questions:

Choose One of the Following Discussion Questions

- What does it mean to be reading the Bible *as literature* in a humanities course as opposed to reading the Bible as a means of religious understanding? What aspects of the text do we notice, discuss, and focus on when we read the Bible as literature? How would the questions that you would ask in English class be different from the ones that you would ask in a Sunday school class? How would the questions that you would ask in English class be different from those of a social studies class?

♦ Compare and contrast the psalms to the stories. How do you personally respond to the Psalms as opposed to the stories? Which brings a closer or more interesting meaning to you? Why? How would you characterize the language in the psalms as opposed to the language of the stories? How does language play a role in your response to each?

♦ Literature, especially poetry, relies heavily on *contrast* to create dramatic interest. Find as many examples as you can of contrast in the selections that we have read. How do these contrasts operate to enhance or clarify the meaning?

♦ When we wrote our poems and descriptions, we learned how to apply various language concepts. Find specific examples from our readings that apply these concepts:

- Specificity (noun sharpening)
- Anglo Saxon verbs
- Metaphor
- Rhythm/refrain
- Onomatopoeia
- Minimizing modifiers
- Unified mood

Differentiation and Technology

Mrs. Daniels arranged the groups by asking students to give their first and second choices, and then assigning students to groups that she thought would work productively together, balancing cognitive abilities and social tendencies.

Everyone read the same texts originally, and then added to that with their Internet research. Students came to these readings with varying levels of prior knowledge. Incidentally, one student, Nate, the only African-American student in this class and one of the few in this school, found his moment in the spotlight in this lesson. Because he attended a Baptist church regularly, his knowledge of the Bible was far greater than that of the other students, most of whom were Catholic or Jewish. Mrs. Daniels was very gratified to see Nate's high level of participation and the astonishment of his classmates when he could rattle off Biblical text, something no one else in the class, including Mrs. Daniels, could do.

References

Benjamin, Amy. (2002). *Differentiated Instruction: A Guide for Middle and High School Teachers*. Larchmont, NY: Eye On Education.

Bernhardt, Victoria. (2000). *Designing and Using Databases for School Improvement*. Larchmont, NY: Eye On Education.

Caine, Renate Nummela, & Caine, Geoffrey. (1994) *Making Connections: Teaching and the Human Brain*. Reading, MA: Addison-Wesley.

Gardner, Howard. (1983). *Multiple Intelligences: The Theory in Practice*. New York: Basic Books.

Tomlinson, Carol Ann. (1999). *The Differentiated Classroom: Responding to the Needs of all Learners*. Alexandria, VA: Association for Supervision and Curriculum Development.

Bibliography

Brooks, Jacqueline, & Brooks, Marton. (1993). *In Search of Understanding: The Case for Constructivist Classrooms*. Alexandria, VA: Association for Supervision and Curriculum Development.

Burke, Jim. (2002). *Tools for Thought*. Portsmouth, NH: Heinemann.

Campbell, Don. (1998). *The Mozart Effect*. New York: Avon.

Fogarty, R. (1998). *Problem-Based learning & Other Curricular Models for the Multiple Intelligences Clasroom*. Arlington Heights, IL: Skylight.

Fogarty, R. (1997). Brain Compatible Classrooms. Arlington Height, IL: Skylight.

Firek, Hilve. (2003). *10 Easy Ways to Use Technology in the English Classroom*. Portsmouth, NH: Heinnemann.

Gregory, Gayle H., & Chapman, Carolyn. (2002). *Differentiated Instructional Strategies: One Size Doesn't Fit All*. Thousand Oaks, CA: Corwin Press.

Lohr, Linda. (2003) *Creating Graphics for Learning and Performanc: Lessons in Visual Literacy*. Upper Saddle River, NJ: Merrill.

Marzano, R.J., Pickering, D.J., & Pollack, J.E. (2000). *Classroom Instruction That Works*. Alexander, WA: Association for Supervision and Curriculum Development.

The Neglected 'R': The Need for a Writing Revolution. (2002). National Commission of Writing in America's Schools and Colleges. The College Board.

Von Blanckensee, Leni. (1999). *Technology Tools for Young Learners.* Larchmont, NY: Eye On Education.

Wahl, Mark. (1999). *Math for Humans*. Langley, WA: LivnLern Press.

Internet Resources

To access this Hotlist of recommended Internet sources, go to www.filamentality.com and search for "DI Using Technology."

Appendix

Appendix I: Grants for Technology in Education

Here is a list of institutions that offer grants that will put computers in your classroom and train you to teach with them:

- Toshiba America Foundation
  http://www.taf.toshiba.com

- The Toyota Tapestry Grant for Teachers:
  http://www.nsta.org/programs/tapestry/index.htm

- Intel
  http://www.intel.com/education/sections/corporate3/index.htm

- U.S. Department of Education Technology Grant Programs
  http://www.ed.gov/about/offices/list/os/technology/edgrants.html

- e-School News Online
  http://www.eschoolnews.com/resources/funding/

- Grant Opportunities
  http://www.schoolgrants.org/grant_opps.htm

- Grant resource for Education Technology Leaders
  http://www.techlearning.com/grants.html

- National Geographic Society Education Foundation Teacher Grants
  http://www.nationalgeographic.com/education/teacher_community/get_grant.html

- U.S. Department of Education Grant Awards
  http://web99.ed.gov/grant/grtawd00.nsf

Hotlinks for How to Write a Grant Proposal

- How to write Grant Proposals
  http://www.seirtec.org/proposaltips/slideshow/index.html

- A Proposal Writing Short Course
  http://www.fdncenter.org/learn/shortcourse/prop1.html

- Grant-Writing Tips
  http://www.schoolgrants.org/tips.htm

- Grant-Writing and Finding Grants
  http://www.grantstech.com/

- Secondary School Teachers Grant Writing Tips
  http://7-12educators.about.com/cs/grantwriting

- Writing and Winning Grants: A Web Tour
  http://techlearning.com/db_area/archives/TL/200106/webtour.html

- Deconstructing a Grant
  http://techlearning.com/db_area/archives/TL/200106/deconstruct.html

- Grant Funding Success Stories
  http://techlearning.com/db_area/archives/TL/2003/06/funding.html

Here are some sources that provide research to support the use of technology in the classroom:

- NSF Educational Technology Workshop
  http://www.cc.gatech.edu/gvu/edtech/nsfws/

- Thirteen/WNET's Concept to Classroom
  http://www.thirteen.org/edonline/concept2class/month4/index_sub2.html

- Apple Classrooms of Tomorrow (ACOT)
  http://www.apple.com/education/k12/leadership/acot/library.html

- Getting Americas Students ready for the 21st Century
  http://www.ed.gov/about/offices/list/os/technology/plan/index.html?exp=0

- e-Learning: Putting a World Class Education at the Fingertips of All Children
  http://www.ed.gov/about/offices/list/os/technology/reports/e-learning.html

Appendix 2: ThinkQuest: www.thinkquest.org

What is ThinkQuest?

ThinkQuest is an international Web site–building competition, sponsored by the Oracle Education Foundation. Teams of students and teachers are challenged to build Web sites on educational topics. These Web sites are published in the popular ThinkQuest Library and top-scoring teams win valuable prizes.

About the Competition:

Competitions begin every 6 months and are open to students and teachers from anywhere in the world. Teams must have 3 to 6 students who are between the ages of 9 and 19, and one adult Coach who is a teacher. To get started, Coaches must enroll their team(s).

Teams have 6 months to build a creative and educational website on any topic within one of the official competition categories. Web sites that show collaboration among team members in more than one school, community, or country are encouraged, and eligible for bonus points.

Entries are evaluated in a two-step process that includes peer review and judging by an international panel of professional educators.

Completed Web sites are published in the ThinkQuest Library for the world to see! In addition, winning teams will travel to the annual ThinkQuest Live event in San Francisco, California.

Join the 25,000 students worldwide who have competed in ThinkQuest since 1996.

Appendix 3:
Handhelds, Gadgets, Gizmos

You may have heard of handheld computers called PDA's (Personal Digital Assistants) or called Palms or Blackberries. Handhelds are perfect for collecting data and taking notes during a field research project. If you are relatively new to using the other technology described in this book, you should establish a comfort level with regular computers first, and then consider the world of handhelds and how they can enhance your classroom.

The most obvious advantage to handhelds is their affordability and convenience. However, along with that advantage is the disadvantage that when students have handhelds, you can't monitor their off-task activities. Handhelds can make you long for the days of yore when students passed physical rather than virtual notes to each other. Another disadvantage of the small size of handhelds is that they are easily lost or stolen. And the glass façade breaks easily in the student's backpack or pocket.

However, handhelds are now a part of our student's world, and are therefore a part of our world as educators. Here are some of the many uses of handhelds in education:

◆ Taking notes and beaming to shared resources

◆ Collecting data and making calculations; taking and recording measurements

◆ Reference tables and other sources of information needed in the field

◆ Personal time and resource management; personal organization

◆ Photography

◆ Text Messaging

◆ Communication

◆ Dictionaries, translators

◆ Handwriters

◆ Teacher administrative tasks

Appendix 4:
15 Independent Computer-Based Activities

The following are productive computer-based activities that students can choose to do if they finish early, need enrichment, or just want to take a break:

- Put together a Hotlist based on an open-ended question to our current topic

- Do a Hotlist search on Filamentality, and turn an existing Hotlist into a WebQuest by turning the topic into a scenario that poses a question.

- Create a digital scrapbook on our current topic.

- Participate in a listserv discussion about our current topic.

- Investigate how other teachers in other schools are learning our current topic. Make suggestions for your teacher.

- Use Quia (www.quia.com) to compose quizzes, puzzles, and games on our current topic.

- Enter an original WebQuest for ThinkQuest.

- Illustrate our current topic with ClipArt.

- Go on a virtual field trip related to our current topic.

- Engage in an Instant Message conversation with another student in the class and print it out.

- Make a Power Point or Hyperstudio presentation on our current topic. Include video and music clips.

- Work on your Web site

- Suggest features for the class Web site

- Find a cool screen saver or wallpaper that relates to our current topic.

- Make cartoon characters that relate to our current topic

Appendix 5: Best Use of Video

"Just Press Play" is not the best use of class time, in my opinion. Given the amount of time students spend in front of television at home, I do find it hard to justify having them spend class time that way except to view videos that they cannot access outside of school. Even then, I believe that videos should be carefully integrated into the Standards, and that students should have preparation and follow-up when videos are shown in class.

That said however, this chapter is about how to make video production and video viewing an effective part of differentiated instruction. What are the alternatives to sitting students in front of a wheel-in video cart and telling them all period to pay attention and stop tipping back on their chairs?

- ◆ *Clips*: Instead of showing the entire movie, some teachers are putting clips together on DVDs. A montage of clips shows juxtaposition and perspective. For example, if you were to show clips of "Glory" juxtaposed with clips of "Gone With the Wind," you'd have an interesting lesson in how the Civil War can be portrayed. My colleague Suzanne Schneider has put together a montage of key scenes in three movie versions of *Romeo and Juliet*. To differentiate instruction, you can have students put together their own theme-based montages.

- ◆ *Students Go to Hollywood*: Many students love to make videos and show them to the class. I have found these to be hilarious, but not necessarily substantial. If you have students make a video, give them a rubric that holds them accountable for content, as well as amusement.

- ◆ *Students in Jeopardy*: The quiz show format is great fun and can be a genuine learning experience. Students should submit written questions, that can be evaluated, to you.

- ◆ *Talking Trash*: Students certainly are familiar with the afternoon court programs and talk show genres. They can adapt various historical and literary arguments to this genre, and they love to do that. Again, though, they need a rubric to anchor them into content.

Learning through watching and producing video is certainly brain compatible and comports with multiple intelligence pedagogy; however, such projects can easily spin out of control. Leading actors are unavailable at key times, equipment fails, things just take longer than expected and if it's on your class time, you'll feel the clock. Video production is best done as homework, one of several unit menu choices.

Videoconferencing

Videoconferencing is like a phone conversation with multiple people who can see as well as hear each other. Right now, videoconferencing requires special telephone and computer equipment, which is available to only a few schools, so videoconferencing has not begun to meet its potential for students. More information about videoconferencing can be found on the Pacific Bell Knowledge Network Explorer Web site (http://www.kn.pacbel.com) and at Global Schoolhouse Web site (http://www.gsn.org)

If you do have the capability for videoconferencing, here are some ways to use it to differentiate instruction:

- Set up a videoconference with other schools to hold a debate, exchange information about a project, hold book club meetings, work collaboratively on a complex project.

- Set up a videoconference with a public official and have a town meeting.

- Set up a multicultural videoconference to discuss current events.

- Set up a videoconference with people overseas in the military.

- Set up a videoconference to hold math competitions with another school.

- Set up a "meet the author" videoconference.

- Set up a videoconference with docents of museums.

- Set up a videoconference relationship with a veterinarian and have the students watch surgeries on animals.

Appendix 6:
Library of Blue Ribbon Learning Sites

http://www.kn.pacbell.com/wired/bluewebn/

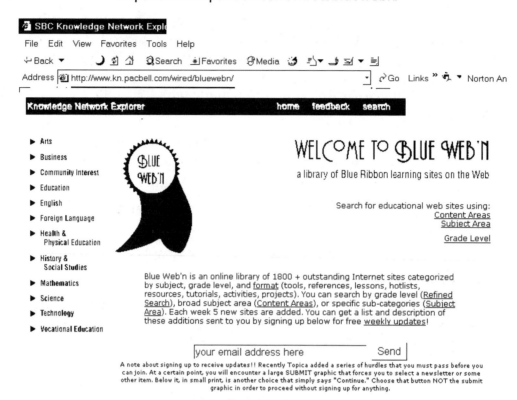

Blue Web'n is an online library of 1800 + outstanding Internet sites categorized by subject, grade level, and format (tools, references, lessons, hotlists, resources, tutorials, activities, projects). You can search by grade level (Refined Search), broad subject area (Content Areas), or specific sub-categories (Subject Area). Each week 5 new sites are added. You can get a list and description of these additions sent to you by signing up below for free weekly updates!

your email address here   Send

A note about signing up to receive updates!! Recently Topica added a series of hurdles that you must pass before you can join. At a certain point, you will encounter a large SUBMIT graphic that forces you to select a newsletter or some other item. Below it, in small print, is another choice that simply says "Continue." Choose that button NOT the submit graphic in order to proceed without signing up for anything.

ABOUT THIS SITE   SEARCH   BROWSE   WEEKLY UPDATES   HOT SITE   SUGGEST A LINK

BLUE WEB'N Content Areas

	Tools	References	Lesson Plans	Hotlists	Information	Resources	Tutorials	Activities	Projects
Arts	14	9	47	29	189		15	84	6
Business	1	2	10	8	39		5	17	1
Community Interest	47	74	33	40	284		16	91	10
Education	36	17	80	55	338		22	79	29
English	10	10	39	30	194		9	118	15
Foreign Language	3	7	9	11	48		5	24	1
Health & Physical Education	3	8	13	21	104		2	39	5
History & Social Studies	17	47	106	55	521		3	223	36
Mathematics	19	5	36	18	95		8	80	18
Science	15	31	120	39	432		22	234	68
Technology (Applied Science)	30	15	13	20	154		28	30	13
Vocational Education	1	8	18	5	77		9	35	2

Quick Search: enter one or two key words here   SEARCH

Create your own online learning resources using
Filamentality

Appendix 7:
Working the Web for Education:
Activity Formats

An Article by Tom March,
a Key Developer of Web Questing
and Founder of Web-n-Flow.com

http://www.web-and-flow.com/help/formats.asp

Background

What follows is one fairly comprehensive strategy for integrating the incredible power of the Internet with student learning. The strategy was first developed by Tom March in the summer of 1996 and developed since. Two new formats have been added for Web-and-Flow users.

The strategy offers easy entry points for newcomers to the Net as well as more sophisticated activities for advanced users. The six formats also take into consideration and many of the promising learning practices suggested by a review of the literature.

This article describes each format, suggests a rationale for why you might choose one format over another, and links to examples.

Introduction

Once you've poked around the Web yourself, and guided students by using a Hotlist, you might want to use the Web to create a goal-based learning activity. Let's say you want to revise a unit because some aspect's not helping students as well as it could. Maybe you now have good access to the Internet and really want to take advantage of this new resource. Or you're just one of those educators who's always trying new things. Good on you.

After all, whenever you develop new curriculum, you have to do some research, brainstorm, locate resources, create handouts, duplicate handouts, stand in line to duplicate handouts, etc. All this could be done using Web-and-Flow to work up an activity. So why not put the whole activity on the Web, not just the links you'll be using (as in a Hotlist).

This way your students can access the complete activity from anywhere, and other teachers and students studying this topic across the world could have access to your learning experience.

The main difference between Hotlists and the other formats is that with Hotlists you send students to Web sites hoping they will find something useful and subsequently create some cognitive sparks. With the other five formats, you choose the format that best meets the needs of the students. In short it works this way:

hotlist   hunt   sampler   reflector   builder   WebQuest

Take a tour through the descriptions and examples by either clicking on the format that addresses your learning goals or reading through the text below.

Topic Hotlist—for Open Research and Exploration

Teachers choose to create a Topic Hotlist when...

♦ they are new to the Web

♦ they are in a hurry

♦ they want to save student surf/search time

♦ they want to add Web resources to curriculum they already have

Background

The natural place to begin integrating the Web for learning is collecting sites that you find most useful/interesting/peculiar on your topic. Doing this will save your learners hours of aimless surfing. In the bad old Pre-Web days, people collected Internet locations on index cards, in databases, or on crumpled scraps of paper. With today's Web browsers, this Internet harvesting can be done through bookmarking your favorite sites with a simple pull down on the menu. This is fine for the machine you're using, but it's a bit of a hassle to get those bookmarks transferred to all the computers in a lab. It's a much more efficient process to create a Web page that collects the locations in a Topic Hotlist. This solves the computer-specific nature of bookmarks and also makes your collection available to everyone in your school, district and the world (nothing like maximizing your effort!).

The Scrapbook Variation

Many technology-using teachers help students create multimedia products as part of the learning process. Students create newsletters, desktop slide presentations, HyperStudio stacks, etc. Before the Web, multimedia content was limited to CD-ROM and what could be scanned or digitized. With the Web, many sites allow and encourage people to use their content for non-profit educational purposes (it's best to check the copyright policy or the site and / or make contact via email). A multimedia Hotlist provides links to a variety of content types such as photographs, maps, stories, facts, quotations, sound clips, videos, virtual reality tours, etc. Learners use the Hotlist links to explore aspects of the topic that they feel are important. They then download or copy and paste these scraps using a variety of software programs. The students' creations will now be richer and more sophisticated because of resources that had never been available in their classrooms before. Also, by allowing students to pursue their own interests amid an abundance of choices, the multimedia Hotlist offers a more open, student-centered approach that encourages construction of meaning. Even though Hotlists don't target specific learning goals, the cluey teacher will use Hotlists to promote the constructivist learning that can happen when students synthesize a large and contextually rich selection of data and experiences.

Tips for Using Hotlists

When you create a Topic Hotlist, your learners will be spared hours of fruitless searching. This is analogous to when a diligent librarian gathers key works from the stacks on a topic your classes are studying, then rolls the books into your room for students to explore. Web resources likely differ in quality, currency, and quirkiness, but the learning strategy is similar: give the students a breadth of materials on the topic they are studying. Excellent learning strategies to invoke now come from the work of Jamie McKenzie (**fromnowon.org**) or Mike Eisenberg and Robert E. Berkowitz (**Big 6 Skills**).

Notice that what's missing is the exact learning you'd like the students to achieve. Those tasks and instructions are probably on the handout they're working from, not the Web page they're using to gain insights, experiences, and information. This is why a Topic Hotlist is an easy strategy to employ; you simply add the Web resources to an activity or unit you already have prepared.

Sometimes you might choose to have learners search their own sites on the Internet. Good examples of this are when students do independent study projects like I-Searches or you have groups studying different aspects of a larger topic (an example would be an interdisciplinary study with student teams each taking a decade in 20th Century American history). In these cases it makes sense to have students search - and post what they have found on the Web via their own hotlist. Whether to prepare a Hotlist for students or let them create their own is probably determined by how many computers you have available to students (in school, in their homes, local libraries, etc.) and available time. Access speed can also cramp student hotlisting if your connection is dial-up, dodgey or molasses.

Examples

- ◆ Topic Hotlist—China on the Net
- ◆ Multimedia Hotlist —Exploring China—Scrapbook

Knowledge Hunt–for Acquiring Defined Knowledge

Teachers choose to create a Knowledge Hunt when…

- ◆ students need to acquire a specific body of knowledge
- ◆ critical thinking is either not a goal is covered using other activities
- ◆ Web-based resources are more current or reliable than traditional resources

Background

Many teachers and librarians who are new to the Web see it as a huge encyclopedia. Subsequently, their first thought is to use the Web for researching and gathering information. Helping students to acquiring knowledge also tends to be one of the main drives in education. Thus it makes sense to create a Web activity structure to meet these goals. The Knowledge Hunt is designed to help students acquire a body of knowledge via the Web.

This said, the Knowledge Hunt sounds like it should be the most used activity format. However, if you view the Web as an encyclopedia, you're due for a rude awakening. Read **3 Myths about the Net** before going any further. Also, knowledge acquisition is just one kind of learning (and a lower level one at that, too). Let's learn more…

Tips for Using Knowledge Hunts

When it's time to develop some solid knowledge on a subject, teachers can create Knowledge Hunts. The basic strategy is to find Web pages that hold information (text, graphic, sound, video, etc.) that you feel is essential to understanding the given topic. Maybe you gather 10 - 15 links (and remember, these are the exact pages you want the students to go to for information, not the top page of a huge Web site). After you've gathered these links, you pose one key question for each Web site you've linked to. In this way, teachers guide students to useful pages and also prompt students to look for information that teachers feel is critical to developing a body of knowledge in the topic.

A smartly designed Knowledge Hunt can go far beyond finding unrelated factoids. By choosing questions that define the scope or parameters of the topic, when the students discover the answers they are tapping into a deeper vein of thought, one that now stakes out the dimensions or schema of the domain being studied. Finally, by including a culminating "Big Question," students can synthesize what they have learned and shape it into a broader understanding of the big picture.

So the Knowledge Hunt is here as one useful strategy to integrate the Web with student learning. However, because of the sketchy verity of very many Web pages (and thus their usefulness for concept development or critical thinking), knowledge acquisition shouldn't be the main use of the Web.

Example Knowledge Hunt—The Treasures of China

Subject Sampler—for Connecting Emotively/Affectively to a Topic

Teachers choose to create a Subject Sampler when...

♦ you want students to feel connected to the topic

♦ you want to motivate students to explore the topic further

♦ you have a short period of time and a small number of great sites to share

♦ you or your students are new to the Web and a user-friendly activity makes sense

Background

Part of what makes the Internet so great is the quirky, passionate, real stuff that many people and organizations post there. You'll find things on the Web that you'd never find on TV, the newspapers, or magazines. Subject Samplers tap into this vibrant vein in order to connect students emotionally to the chosen topic. Specifically, Samplers work like those chocolate samplers: you open the box, look things over, think you see something you'd like, then poke your finger into it. If you like it, you eat it. If you don't, you leave it pre-poked for someone else's taste.

Tips for Using Subject Samplers

Specifically, in a Subject Sampler learners are presented with a smaller number (maybe half a dozen) of intriguing Web sites organized around a main topic. What makes this a particularly effective way to engage student buy-in is that first off, you've chosen Web sites themselves that offer something interesting to do, read, or see. Second, students are asked to respond to the Web-based activities from a personal perspective. Rather than uncover hard knowledge (as they do in a Knowledge Hunt), students are asked about their perspectives on topics, comparisons to experiences they have had, personal interpretations of artworks or data, etc. Thus, more important than the right answer is that students are invited to join the community of learners surrounding the topic, for students to see that their views are valued in this context.

Example: Subject Sampler—My China

Insight Reflector—for Prompting Open Reflection

Teachers choose to create a Insight Reflector when…

♦ creative thinking is more important than a uniform response

♦ the subject matter benefits from being viewed through new perspectives

♦ you want students to engage their emotions and minds in the topic

♦ reflective writing is a course objective

Background

A higher-level cognitive skill valued by many state curricula and standards is reflective thinking and writing. In brief, this is the kind of creative mental pondering that reveals a mind at work. It's the open processing of an intriguing stimuli through a person's experience, ideas, and emotions. It brings all aspects of the person's nature to the task of making sense of the stimuli. While a highly valued skill, it's also a very difficult thing to teach.

Again, the wealth of the Web can assist us here. The first aspect of reflective writing is an opening occasion, something that sparks an emotion or starts the mental gears to turn. With its abundance of special interests and overt agendas, the Web affords more chances for reflection than are usually found in a classroom. Teachers gather a page or pages from the Web that they feel will perturb learners in such a way as to create a positive dissonance, then prompt students to look at the topic in different ways, to mull things over, to chew their cog(itations).

Tips for Using Insight Reflectors

Insight Reflectors won't be something you'll use as frequently as Subject Samplers or WebQuests, but when encouraging a creative thinking process is more important than prompting one defined and uniform outcome from students, try prompting insights with the Reflector. English and social studies classes as well as ethical approaches to science and technology are typical applications of the format.

Example: Insight Reflector—The Otherness of the Past

Concept Builder—for Developing and Refining New Concepts

Teachers choose to create a Concept Builder when…

♦ a simple definition is too abstract

♦ examples of the concept are available on the Web

♦ at least a few critical attributes of the concept are easily perceived

♦ you want to engage students in higher level thinking

Background

Another aspect of the Web that makes it a rich learning resource is the breadth of examples available. On almost any given topic, people have posted either professional or homespun pages sharing their information and perspectives. This maps very well to how we learn concepts: by viewing many examples we can derive the critical attributes or essential elements that define an "Impressionist painting," "cumulonimbus clouds," "social revolutions." Because conceptualizing is a higher level thinking skill that takes root in students' pre-existing schemas and requires an ongoing process of refinement, direct instruction of concepts is often an exercise in frustration for everyone. A better way might be to show students an array of well-selected examples and let them build or construct the concepts for themselves, then subsequent class discussions can help everyone refine their thinking.

Tips for Using Concept Builders

When learning the definition of a class of things (artistic eras, types of clouds, social upheavals, etc.) doesn't fully capture the subtleties you want students to appreciate and distinguish, then you'd better help them move beyond concrete definitions into the fuzzier realm that requires an engaged mind to discern key characteristics and argue interpretations. Gray areas? Yes, but fun as all get-out in the classroom (as long as everyone sees this as a process, not a right answer). So when you have a good supply of Web sites that show examples of a concept that's valuable for students to learn, link to at least three sample sites, then offer a series of short questions that prompt them to look for specific details and comparisons and contrasts. Depending on the concept, the examples, and the learners, you may lead them very far with your prompts or let them do some problem-based learning by not using prompts at all. Furthermore, by linking to additional resources, students could do even more independent research. After the activity, you might test the students concepts as a group with some "non-examples" (expressionist paintings, cumulo-stratus clouds, evolutionary changes in societies). Lastly, because images are good sources of information and are becoming more common and quicker loading all the time on the Web, Concept Builders make a good higher-level thinking activity to support younger or non-reading students.

Example: Concept Builder—No Fear o' Eras (from **Eyes on Art 2.0**)

WebQuest—for Engaging in Critical Thinking

Teachers choose to create a WebQuest when…

+ you want students to tackle big, complex, or gray questions
+ students could benefit from cooperative learning
+ the subject warrants a deeper understanding
+ students would benefit from a more real world learning experience

Background

When it's time to go beyond learning facts, connecting emotively, or developing concepts, to put all these together and get into the grayer matter, your students are ready for a WebQuest. Basically, a WebQuest is an inquiry activity that presents student groups with a central Question and related Task. Access to the Web (and other resources) provides abundant grist from which collaborative student groups construct meaning. The whole learning process is supported by prompting/scaffolds to promote higher-order thinking. The products of WebQuests are usually then put out to the world for some type of real feedback.

Tips for Using WebQuests

When designing a WebQuest it's best to choose a topic that's either large, complex or in dispute. Current events, social issues, and environmental systems, etc. all work well. Also anything that requires evaluation or scientific hypothesizing will evoke a variety of interpretations. The reason the Web is so critical is because it offers the breadth of perspectives and viewpoints that are usually needed to construct meaning on complex topics. Students benefit from being linked to a wide variety of Web resources so that they can explore and make sense of the issues involved in the challenge.

Logistically, all students begin by learning some common background knowledge, then divide into groups. In the groups each student or pair of students have a particular role, task, or perspective to master. They effectively become experts on one aspect of a topic. When the roles come together, students must synthesize their learning by completing a transformative task such as e-mailing congressional representatives or presenting their interpretation to real world experts on the topic.

You might want to use an WebQuest as a first activity to quickly immerse students in real learning, then go back and fill in the broader picture with a Knowledge Hunt or Subject Sampler.

Example: WebQuest—Tuskegee Tragedy

Presented: November 20, 1996, Classroom Connect Conference, Anaheim; Published: April 20, 1998, Computer-Using Educators Newsletter; Revised: October 24, 2001, for Web-and-Flow Interactive. © 1999–2003 Web-and-Flow